B'ajlom ii Nkotz'i'j P

Judeo-Spanish Phrasebook:

Ideal for Traveling within Sephardic Jewish Communities around the World

Mateo Russo and Sandra Chigüela

1st Edition

(2023)

B'ajlom ii Nkotz'i'j Publications'

Judeo-Spanish Phrasebook:

Ideal for Traveling within Sephardic Jewish Communities around the World

First Edition (2023)

THIS BOOK IS DEDICATED TO MY WIFE, SANDRA, AND OUR FIVE CHILDREN: CRISTEL, EMILIO, ALEJANDRA, CAMILA, AND GALILEA

WE WOULD ALSO LIKE TO GIVE A SPECIAL THANKS TO URIEL MEDINA. WITHOUT HIM THIS BOOK NEVER WOULD HAVE BEEN CREATED.

Brief History of the Author

Mateo Russo and his wife Sandra founded 'Bajlom ii Nkotz'i'j Publications' in 2018. The organization was named using two words of Mayan origin from the Tz'utujiil Language of Guatemala. The two words tell the love story of Mateo and Sandra. 'B'ajlom' means 'Jaguar' and the word 'Nkotz'i'j' means 'My flower' which is the loving name that Mateo gave to his wife. This love story of the Jaguar and his beloved flower gave birth to the mission of Mateo to preserve indigenous languages of Guatemala and southern Mexico and to create linguistic texts that can provide a written record of specific dialects and the stories of people who are collaborators with this project. The goal is to preserve all of the indigenous languages of Guatemala and others from southern Mexico; not only through a text book or grammar book, but through poetry, songs, and many other forms of literary art and artistic expression. The goal is to give a voice to the highly marginalized indigenous people who have been highly discriminated against in all societies of Latin America. Mateo has hopes in expanding this project through time, one language at a time. Mateo's philosophy is founded in the philosophy of EZLN (The Zapatista Army of National Liberation) and through the teachings of Subcomandante Marcos the original spokesperson for EZLN. The fight of EZLN has inspired Mateo to create another front in the fight that continues: The battle to preserve and protect the remnants of our past and our perception of the world around us, our own words and those words being of our ancestors. Our indigenous linguistic history is very beautiful and it needs to be preserved, because it is our linguistic inheritance. Despite that many indigenous languages are moribund... Mateo and his wife have joined together with the fight to preserve the most important facet of the cultures of the indigenous people: Our linguistic inheritance (our mother tongues). Mateo passionately supports Indigenous Human Rights and the preservation and protection of every indigenous language of Guatemala and southern Mexico. Mateo will not rest until every indigenous language has a written literary archive and until the voice of the indigenous people is not forgotten but is permanently marked in human history.

Contact Information:

'B'ajlom ii Nkotz'i'j Publications'

biinpublications@gmail.com

biinpublications@facebook.com

If you would like to donate to our cause and give your support or if you would like to donate your time or be a literary collaborator with us, please, contact us by e-mail.

Table of Contents:

ג׳ודיאו-איספאנייול

לאדינו

DJUDEO-ESPANYOL

LADINO

JUDEO-SPANISH

LADINO

Text book with Grammar, a Dictionary,

and Daily Useful Phrases

Part I: A Brief Grammar of the Judeo-Spanish Language (Djudeo-espanyol)

Judaeo-Spanish or Judeo-Spanish - Hebrew [ג׳ודיאו-איספאנייול], Cyrillic [жудеоеспањол], Latin [Djudeo-espanyol]; also known as Ladino [לאדינו], is a Romance Language derived from Old Spanish. Originally spoken in Spain, and then after the Edict of Expulsion spreading through the Ottoman Empire (Balkans, Turkey, Western Asia, and North Africa) as well as France, Italy, the Netherlands, Morocco, and England, it is today spoken mainly by Sephardic minorities in more than 30 countries, with most speakers residing in Israel. Although it has no official status in any country, it has been acknowledged as a minority language in Bosnia and Herzegovina, Israel, France, and Turkey. In 2017, it was formally recognized by the Royal Spanish Academy.

The core vocabulary of Judeo-Spanish is Old Spanish, and it has numerous elements from the other old Romance Languages of the Iberian Peninsula: Old Aragonese, Astur-Leonese, Old Catalan, Galician-Portuguese, and Mozarabic. The language has been further enriched by Ottoman Turkish and Semitic vocabulary, such as Hebrew, Aramaic, and Arabic – especially in the domains of religion, law, and spirituality – and most of the vocabulary for new and modern concepts has been adopted through French and Italian. Furthermore, the language is influenced to a lesser degree by other local languages of the Balkans, such as Greek, Bulgarian, and Serbo-Croatian.

Historically, the Rashi script and its cursive form Solitreo have been the main orthographies for writing Judeo-Spanish. However, today it is mainly written with the Latin alphabet, though some other alphabets such as Hebrew and Cyrillic are still in use. Judeo-Spanish has been known also by other names, such as: Español (Espanyol. Spaniol, Spaniolish, Espanioliko), Judió (Judyo, Djudyo) or Jidió (Jidyo, Djidyo), Judesmo (Judezmo, Djudezmo), Sefaradhí (Sefaradí) or Haketía (in North Africa). In Turkey, and formerly in the Ottoman Empire, it has been traditionally called *Yahudice* in Turkish, meaning the 'Jewish

11

Language.' In Israel, Hebrew speakers usually call the language Espanyolit, Spanyolit, and only in recent years, Ladino.

Judeo-Spanish, once the Jewish Trade Language of the Adriatic Sea, the Balkans, and the Middle-East, and renowned for its rich literature, especially in Salonika, today is under serious threat of extinction. Most native speakers are elderly, and the language is not transmitted to their children or grandchildren for various reasons; consequently, all Judeo-Spanish-speaking communities are undergoing a language shift. In some expatriate communities in Spain, Latin America, and elsewhere, there is a threat of assimilation by modern Spanish. It is experiencing, however, a minor revival among Sephardic communities, especially in music.

In recent decades in Israel, followed by the United States and Spain, the language has come to be referred to as Ladino, literally meaning 'Latin.' This name for the language was promoted by a body called the Autoridad Nasionala del Ladino, although speakers of the language in Israel referred to their mother tongue as Espanyolit or Spanyolit. Native speakers of the language consider the name Ladino to be incorrect; reserving the term for the 'semi-sacred' language used in word-for-word translations from the Bible, which is distinct from the spoken vernacular.

The derivation of the name Ladino is complicated. Before the expulsion of the Jews from Spain, the word meant literary Spanish, as opposed to other dialects or Romance languages in general, as distinct from Arabic.

Judaeo-Spanish Ladino should not be confused with the Ladino or Ladin Language that is spoken in part of Northeastern Italy and which has nothing to do with the Jews or with Spanish beyond being a Romance Language, a property that they share with French, Italian, Portuguese, and Romanian.

At the time of the expulsion from Spain, the day-to-day language of the Jews of different regions of the peninsula was hardly, if at all, different from that of their Christian neighbors, but there may have been some dialect mixing to form a sort of Jewish Lingua Franca. There was, however, a special stye of Spanish used for purposes of study or translation, featuring a more archaic dialect, a large number of Hebrew and Aramaic loanwords, and a tendency to render Hebrew word order literally: Ha-laylah ha-zeh – "this night" was rendered – La noche la esta – "this night" opposed to 'Esta noche.'

Following the Expulsion, the process of dialect mixing continued, but Castilian Spanish remained by far the largest contributor. The daily language was increasingly influenced both by the language of study and by the local non-Jewish vernaculars, such as Greek and Turkish. It came to be known as Judesmo and, in that respect, the development is parallel to that of Yiddish. However, many speakers, especially among the community leaders, also had command of a more formal style, *castellano*, which was nearer to the Spanish at the time of the Expulsion.

SOURCE LANGUAGES:

The following languages played a part in the development of what we today call 'Judeo-Spanish' or 'Ladino.'

Old Spanish
Portuguese
Galician-Portuguese
Old Catalan
Old Astur-Leonese

Asturian

Old Aragonese

Hebrew

Aramaic

Arabic

Ottoman Turkish

Turkish

Serbo-Croatian

Bulgarian

Greek

ALPHABETS:

Rashi script

Modified Hebrew

Cyrillic script

Latin-based (from Spanish)

Latin-based (from English)

The Judeo-Spanish within this Phrasebook will be written in a Latin-based script that previously had been developed for Judeo-Spanish

I)   The   Judeo-Spanish   Alphabet   and   Pronunciation

Judeo-Spanish Alphabet

LATIN SCRIPT

A a   B b   CH ch   D d   Dj dj   E e   F f   G g

H h   I I   J j   K k   L l   M m   N n   Ny ny

O o   P p   R r   S s   Sh sh   T t   U u   V v

X x   Y y   Z z

*27 total letters

*LETTERS 'A, I, O, E' CAN BE ACCENTED: Á, Í, Ó, É

A a = like 'o' in the word 'gobble'

B b = like 'b' in 'boy'

CH ch = like 'ch' in 'church'

D d = like 'd' in 'dad'

Dj dj = like 'j' in 'Japan'

E e = like 'e' in 'bed'

F f = like 'f' in 'fox'

G g = like 'g' in 'goat'

H h = a rough 'h' sound like in the Spanish word 'jalapeño.' This letter is also interchangeable with 'X.' There are times when this letter is used where it is silent. Some parts of this book will use 'Ḥ' to signify that the letter is like a rough 'h'.

I I = like 'ee' in 'beet'

J j = like 's' in 'leisure'

K k = like 'c' in the word 'cat'

L l = like 'l' in 'like'

M m = like 'm' in 'monkey'

N n = like 'n' in 'nut'

Ny ny = like 'ni' in the word 'onion'

O o = like 'oa' in 'boat'

P p = like 'p' in 'push'

R r = like 'r' in 'rabbit;' if this letter is doubles 'rr'
then it is trilled just like in Spanish.

S s = like 's' in 'sweet'

Sh sh = like 'sh' in 'shopping'

T t = like 't' in 'tar'

U u = like 'oo' in 'boot'

V v = like 'v' in 'vineyard'

X x = a rough 'h' very much like 'j' in the Spanish word 'jalapeño.' This word is interchangeable with 'SH' (with some words and not others) and 'H.' This letter can also be pronounced rougher like 'kh'

Y y = like 'y' in the word 'yellow'

Z z = like 'z' in the word 'zebra'

Judeo-Spanish Alphabet

HEBREW SCRIPT

א   [A / E / O, -]

ב   [B]

ב'   [V]

ג   [G]

ג'   [DJ]

ד   [D]

ה   [H]

ו   [U / O / V]

ז   [Z]

ז׳ [J / ZH] sometimes like 'j' in English, but mostly like 's' in the word 'leisure'

ח [Ḥ] pronounced like a rough 'h' (throaty)

ט [T] most commonly used in Judeo-Spanish

י [I / E / Y]

יי [Y]

כ ך [K, H, KH] pronounced like a rough 'h' (throaty)

ל [L]

מ ם [M]

נ ן [N]

נײ [NY]

ס   [S]

ע   [E / A / -]

ף פ   [P]

'ף 'פ   [F]

ץ צ   [TZ] used mostly with words of Hebrew or Aramaic

origin.

ק   [K] most commonly used with Judeo-Spanish

ר   [R]

ש   [SH / S] mostly used for 'sh' but sometimes 's'

ת   [T / TH] used mostly with words of Hebrew or

Aramaic origin.

*28 letters total

Judeo-Spanish Alphabet

CYRILLIC SCRIPT

А а   Б б   В в   Г г   Д д   Е е   Ж ж

[A]   [B]   [V]   [G]   [D]   [E]   [DJ / J]

З з   И и   Й й / J j   К к   Л л   М м   Н н

[Z]   [I]   [Y]   [K]   [L]   [M]   [N]

Њ њ   Љ љ   О о   П п   Р р   С с   Т т

[NY]   [LY]   [O]   [P]   [R]   [S]   [T]

У у   Ф ф   Х х   Ц ц   Ч ч   Ш ш   Я я

[U]   [F]   [H / Ḥ / X]   [TZ]   [CH]   [SH]   [IA]

Rarely used letters:

Ю ю   Э э   Щ щ   Ы ы

[YU / IU]   [E]   [SHCH]   [I / Y]

*33 letters total

26

I (a) <u>Vowels</u>

The Judeo-Spanish language utilizes the following vowels:

A = 'a' like the 'o' in the word 'bottle' - **Á** [long vowel]

E = like 'e' in the word 'bet' – **É** [long vowel]

I = like 'ee' in the word 'beet' – **Í** [long vowel]

O = 'o' like 'oa' in 'boat' – **Ó** [long vowel]

U = 'u' like 'oo' in 'boot'

Hebrew Alphabet Note:

The letters [י] and [ו] are always preceded by [א] and are never shown alone in a word. [א] and [י] are use together for the Spanish sound [ey]

DIPHTHONGS IN JUDEO-SPANISH:

AI / AY [like 'ye' in 'bye!']   **IA** [ee-ah]

AU [like 'ow' in 'owl']   **EO** [ey-oh]

EI / EY [like 'ay' in 'bay']   **EU** [ey-oo]

OI / OY [like 'oy' in 'toy']   **UE** [wey]

UAY [like the word 'why']   **UA** [wah]

CONSONANT ANOMALIES:

CH = [like 'ch' in 'chase']

GU = [hard 'g' before 'e' & 'i' / 'gw' before 'a' & 'o']

NY = [like 'ni' in 'onion']

RR = [trilled 'r' done with the tongue]

X = 'x' usually is like a rough 'h' very much like the letter 'j' in Spanish word 'jalapeño'

Y = Judeo-Spanish uses 'yeísmo' and all words that would have a 'll' [double 'l'] in them become a 'y'

S = the letter 's' is said just like in English, because Judeo-Spanish is a 'seseo' language unlike the Spanish spoken in Spain today.

I)   Personal Pronouns

In this part there are multiple tables; one with personal pronouns, one with pronouns used to denote possession of an object and several that show object pronouns.

Personal Pronouns [Subject of Sentence]

First person singular and plural	YO = I	NOZOTROS(AS) MOZOTROS(AS) MOZÓS(ÁS) = We
Second person singular and plural	TU = You	VOZOTROS(AS) VOZÓS(ÁS) = You
Third person singular and plural	EL, EYA = He, She, It	EYOS, EYAS = They

Ex.

YO ESTO EN LA KOMUNITIKA = I AM IN THE COMMUNITY

VOZÓS ESTASH EN EL KOLLEL = YOU ARE IN THE COMMUNITY

Personal Possession

The following table shows Possessive Pronouns:

1st pers. sing. and plural	MI = my	MUESTRO(A) = our pl
2nd pers. sing. and plural	TU = your	VUESTRO(A) = your pl
3rd pers. sing. and plural	SU = his, her, its	SU = their pl

NOTE: ALL OF THESE FORMS CAN BE MADE PLURAL BY SIMPLY ADDING A '-S'

MIS GATOS = MY CATS

TUS DJUGETES = YOUR TOYS

SUS PALAVRAS = HIS/HER/YOUR/THEIR WORDS

MUESTROS PERROS = OUR DOGS

EXAMPLES WITH A PREPOSITION:

KON (WITH) + PRONOUN

1	KON *MI = With me	KON MOZOTROS KON NOZOTROS = With us
2	KON *TI = With you	KON VOZOTROS = With all of you
3	KON EL / EYA = With him/her/it	KON EYOS / EYAS = With them

1st and 2nd person singular Dative Pronouns are used with prepositions.

Direct Objects #1 – ACCUSATIVE

1	ME = me	NOS / MOS = us
2	TE = you	VOS = you
3	LO / LA =him/her/it	LOS / LAS = them

-Direct objects and indirect objects can be placed together with Imperative Verb Forms or they can appear at the beginning of a sentence back-to-back before the initial verb.

DAMELO! = GIVE ME IT!

TE LO VO A DAR = I AM GOING TO GIVE IT TO YOU

1st & 2nd person plural change when there is a direct and indirect object in the same sentence:

MOS < MO

VOS < VO

Ex.

MO LO DASH = YOU ALL GIVE IT TO US

VO LO VO A DAR = I'M GOING TO GIVE IT TO YOU ALL

3rd person plural changes from a 'LO/LA/LE' to a 'SE' when there are two 3rd person objects in a sentence:

LO / LA / LE / LOS / LAS / LES < SE

Ex.

SE LOS DI = I GAVE THEM TO HIM

SE LOS VO A DAR = I WILL GIVE THEM TO HIM

Indirect Objects #2

1	MI = to me	NOS A NOZOTROS(AS) A MOZOTROS(AS) = to us
2	TI = to you	VOS A VOZOTROS(AS) = to you
3	LE (L') – (SE) = to him/her/it	LES (L') – (SE / SEN[1]) = to them

[1] Infinitive only – Ex. LAVARSEN = To Wash themselves

'**SE**' is used when a Direct Object is coupled with an Indirect Object and both are is 3rd sing. or plural

NO **SE** LO DI = I DID NOT GIVE HIM IT

IT IS NOT POSSIBLE IN JUDEO-SPANISH TO SAY: NO LE LO DI

NOTE: (L') IS USED WHEN THE VERB BEGINS WITH A VOWEL: SE **L'**AVLI = I SPOKE IT TO HIM

Examples with Pronouns:

I love you = **YO TE** AMO

I want you to help me! =

KERO KE **ME** AYUDES

My name = **MI** NOMBRE

Give it to me! = DA**MELO**!

Come with me! = VENGASE **KON MI**!

I want to go with you =

KERO IR **KON TI**

Do you love me? =

ME AMAS?

This is for her = ESTE ES PARA **EYA**

My arm = **MI** BRAZO

My heart = **MI** KORASON

I will help you = **TE** AYUDARÉ

Do it! = AGALO!

II)   Prepositions

Prepositions are fairly simple in Judeo-Spanish. They do not require the Nouns or Pronouns that come after them to take on any special forms like most 'Case' Languages do; like Russian, Bosnian, Latin and a plethora of other Languages around the world. The following list will show the common Prepositions in the Judeo-Spanish Language.

EN = IN; ON; INTO, AT

SPECIAL FORM: EN + EL (THE) = **ENEL**

ESTOY **EN** LA KAZA = I AM AT HOME

ESTAMOS **ENEL** MIZMO LUGAR = WE ARE IN THE SAME PLACE

VO A IR **EN** AYA = I AM GOING TO GO IN THERE

EN LA MEZA = ON THE TABLE

A = TO; INTO; TOWARDS

SPECIAL FORM: A + EL (THE) = **AL**

VO **A** LA KAZA = I AM GOING HOME

VAMOS **AL** BANKO = WE GO TO THE BANK

GRASIAS **A** VOZÓS! = THANKS TO YOU ALL!

ASTA = UNTIL; UP TO

SOLO ESPERO **ASTA** TENGO KE ENTRAR = I ONLY

AM WAITING UNTIL I HAVE TO ENTER

DE = FROM; OF; OUT OF; ABOUT

SPECIAL FORM: DE + EL (THE) = **DEL**

SOY **DE** LOS ESTADOS UNIDOS = I AM FROM THE UNITED STATES

ALGO **DE** MUEVO = SOMETHING NEW

DE KE FAVLAS TU? = WHAT ARE YOU TALKING ABOUT?

EL GATO **DE** MI ERMANIKO = MY BROTHER'S CAT

KON = WITH

KON KEN AVLÁSH VOZÓS? = WITH WHOM DO YOU SPEAK?

KON MI = WITH ME

KON TI = WITH YOU

CON VOZÓS = WITH YOU

NON FAVLES **KON MI**! = DON'T SPEAK TO ME!

KON MIS AMIGOS = WITH MY FRIENDS

POR = FOR; BECAUSE OF; DUE TO

POR SIEMPRE = FOREVER

POR LA ETERNIDAD = FOR ETERNITY

LE ORASIONAMOS **POR** EYA = WE PRAY FOR HER

PORKE FAVLAS TU ANSI? = WHY ARE YOU SPEAKING LIKE THAT!

PARA = FOR; IN ORDER TO; UNTIL; TO; TOWARDS

PARA TI = FOR YOU

PARA MI = FOR ME

PARA MOZOTROS = FOR US

VO **PARA** AYA = I AM GOING THERE

SALÍ DE AYI **PARA** SIEMPRE = I LEFT FROM THERE FOREVER

VO A AZERLO **PARA** TI = I AM GOING TO DO IT FOR YOU

SIN = WITHOUT

SIN MI = WITHOUT ME

SIN MI ERMANIKO = WITHOUT MY BROTHER

SIN KOMIDA =WITHOUT FOOD

SIN TI = WITHOUT YOU

ANTES (DE) = BEFORE

ANTES DE LA KAYE = BEFORE THE STREET

ANTES DE LA KAZA = BEFORE THE HOME

ANTES DE TI = BEFORE YOU

ANTES DE MI = BEFORE ME

DESPUES / DOSPUES (DE) = AFTER

DOSPUES DE IR A MI KAZA = AFTER GOING TO MY HOUSE

DESPUES DE MI ERMANIKO = AFTER MY BROTHER

DOSPUES DE LAVORAR = AFTER WORKING

ENTRE = BETWEEN

ENTRE MOZOTROS = BETWEEN US

ENTRE LOS ARVOLES = BETWEEN THE TREES

ENTRE LOS DOS OMBRES = BETWEEN THE TWO MEN

DEBASHO (DE); BASHO (DE); ABASHO = UNDER; BELOW; BENEATH; UNDERNEATH

DEBASHO DE MOZOTROS = BELOW US

DEBASHO DE MI = BELOW ME

BASHO DE LA KAZA = UNDER THE HOUSE

DEBASHO DE MI KOCHE = UNDERNEATH MY CAR

ENDRIVA / ENRIVA / SOVRE = ABOVE; OVER

ENDRIVA DE / ENRIVA DE = OVER; ABOVE; ON TOP OF

SOVRE MOZOTROS = ABOVE US

SOVRE LA KAZA = ABOVE THE ROOF

SOVRE MI KOCHE = ABOVE MY CAR

SOVRE MI = ABOVE ME

ENDRIVA DE LA KAZA = ABOVE MY HOUSE

ENRIVA DE MI KOCHE = ABOVE MY CAR

ENSIMA (DE) = OVER; ON TOP OF

ENSIMA DE MI KOCHE = ON TOP OF MY CAR

ENSIMA DE TI = ON TOP OF YOU

ENFRENTE (DE) = IN FRONT OF

ENFRENTE DE TI = IN FRONT OF YOU

ENFRENTE DE MI ERMANIKO = IN FRONT OF MY BROTHER

ENFRENTE DE MI KOCHE = IN FRONT OF MY CAR

ENFRENTE DE MI KAZA = IN FRONT OF THE HOUSE

DETRAS (DE); ATRAS (DE) = BEHIND; AT THE BACK OF

A TU **ATRAS** = BEHIND YOU

DETRAS DE MI ERMANIKO = BEHIND MY BROTHER

DETRAS DE MI KOCHE = BEHIND MY CAR

AL **ATRAS DE** LA KAZA = AT THE BACK OF THE HOUSE

AL LADO (DE); A LADO (DE) = AT THE SIDE OF; NEXT TO

A TU LADO / A TU LADIKO = AT YOUR SIDE

AL LADO DE LA KAZA = AT THE SIDE OF THE HOUSE

SERKA (DE) = NEAR TO; NEXT TO

SERKA DEL EDIFICIO = NEXT TO THE BUILDING

EL ESTA MUY **SERKA** = HE IS NEAR

SERKA DE MI KAZA = NEAR MY HOUSE

LESHOS DE = FAR FROM

LESHOS DE MI KAZA = FAR FROM MY HOUSE

EL ESTA MUY **LESHOS** = HE IS VERY FAR AWAY

VERSO = TOWARDS; IN THE DIRECTION OF

VERSO LA KAZA VAZIYA = TOWARDS THE EMPTY HOUSE

VERSO EL BANKO SERRADO = TOWARDS THE CLOSED BANK

VERSO EL LUGAR FERMOZO = TOWARDS THE BEAUTIFUL PLACE

Examples of Pronouns and Prepositions:

KERES IR **KON MI**?

(Do you want to go with me?)

SE **DE** LOS ESTADOS UNIDOS

(I am from the United States)

BIVO **EN** LOS ESTADOS UNIDOS

(I live in the United States)

KERO IR **AL** SHARSHÍ

(I want to go to the market)

VO **A** LA KAZA

(I am going [to] my home!)

SE LO DI **A** MI ERMANIKO

(I gave it to my brother)

TRAIGA**MELO**!

(Bring it to me!)

TRAELDO **A** LA KAZA!

(Bring it to the house!)

III)   The Noun

Nouns in Judeo-Spanish are either masculine or feminine. Most Masculine nouns end in 'o' or a consonant and most feminine nouns end in 'a.' There of course exceptions to the rules.

Basic nouns:

KOMIDA (Food)

ANIMAL (Animal), ANIMALES (Animals)

KAYE (Road, Path), KAYES (Roads, Paths)

PAN (Bread)

MUJER (Woman), MUJERES (Women)

OMBRE (Man), OMBRES (Men)

NOMBRE (Name), NOMBRES (Names)

BOKA (Mouth), BOKAS (Mouths)

OJO (Eye), OJOS (Eyes)

PALAVRA (Word), PALAVRAS (Words)

*As can be seen above with the examples of nouns and their plurals, all nouns take the ending '-S' in order to form a plural noun. Nouns that end in a consonant receive '-ES' as their plural ending. All nouns are assigned a gender and will have to be memorized.

A General Rule for Determining a Nouns Gender:

- [consonant] (masc.) *usually, but not always:*

ex. La mujer = the woman

-E (masc.) *usually, but not always: ex. La djente = the people*

-O (masc.) *usually, but not always: ex. La mano = the hand*

-A (fem.) *usually, but not always: ex. El sofa = the sofa*

PLURALS:

-S [after vowel] / -ES [after consonant]

If the noun ends in '-S' then the '-S' becomes a 'Z' followed by '-ES'

Ex.

MES [month] < MEZES [months]

If a noun has an accent mark towards the end of a word, then in the plural the accent mark is removed:

Ex.

LIMÓN [lemon] < LIMONES [lemons]

MATRAPÁS   [middle-man]   <   MATRAPAZES [middlemen]

Words of Hebrew origin can receive Hebrew endings or Spanish plural ending:

Ex.

KAL [Synagogue] < KALIM or KALES

KAHAL [Synagogue] < KAHALIM or KAHALES

KEHILÁ [Synagogue] < KEHILOT or KEHILAS

KEILÁ [Synagogue] < KEILOT or KEILOT

And some words of Old Spanish Origin can receive Hebrew endings as well:

Ex.

ERMANO [brother] < ERMANIM or ERMANOS

ERMANA [sister] < ERMANOT or ERMANAS

HEBREW WORDS IN JUDEO-SPANISH:

Judeo-Spanish has a plethora of Hebrew vocabulary mixed with a plethora of words from other languages. The following will be examples of how to form and properly pronounc Hebrew Loanwords in Judeo-Spanish.

*All Hebrew words are spelled in the same way as they are in Hebrew. Only the pronunctiation may change following these several criteria:

קהל [QAḤAL] < [KAHAL / KAḤAL]

SYNAGOGUE

As one can see the vowels are intact. The 'Qoph' becomes a regular 'k' sound in Ladino. The 'Heth' becomes a regular rough 'h' sound like in Spanish.

קהלים [QAḤALIM] < [KAHALIM / KAḤALIM]

Here is the same word, yet in the plural with a Hebrew plural ending.

ברכה [BƏRAKHÁH] < [BERAXÁ]

BLESSING

As can be seen with the changes in this feminine Hebrew Loanwoard; 'kh' becomes 'x' in Ladino and is pronounced the same. The final feminine ending becomes a simple long vowel 'a'. The 'schwa' between 'b' and 'r' becomes a letter 'e' in Ladino. This goes for all words with a 'schwa.'

ברכות [BƏRAKHOT] < [BERAXOT]

As with the plural, the feminine ending is the same as in the Hebrew.

מברך [MƏVAREKH] < [MEBAREX]

Here is a participle that means 'one who blesses.' In Ladino it simply means 'Blesser' or 'one who gives blessings.' As can be seen, the same changes occur as shown previously. These types of nouns can receive either a Hebrew male or female singular ending or a Hebrew male or female plural ending.

שדה תעופה [SƏDEH TƏ'UFAH] < [SEDÁ TE'UFÁ]

AIRPORT

Note the changes with this feminine noun with a feminine adjective.

תפילה [TƏFILEH] < [TEFILÁ]

PRAYER

Note the changes in pronunciation. The 'schwa' becomes an 'e' and the final feminine ending becomes a long vowel 'a'

צדקה [TZƏDAQÁH] < [SEDAKÁ]

JUSTICE / CHARITY

Note the changes in pronunciation. The 'Tzadiq' becomes a regular 's' and the 'schwa' becomes an 'e'. The final feminine ending is pronounced like a long vowel 'a' and the 'Qoph' becomes a simple 'k.'

Indefinite Article:

In Judeo-Spanish the Indefinite articles are '**UN** (masc.) / **UNA** (fem.) / **UNOS** (masc. pl) / **UNAS** (fem. pl)' and they always precede the noun.

These forms correspond to the English 'A /AN.'

-UNOS / UNAS = SOME / ANY

UNOS KALEMES = SOME PENCILS

UNAS MUJERES = SOME WOMEN

UN LIVROS = A BOOK

UN KUCHILYO = A KNIFE

UN GATO = A CAT

UN PERRO = A DOG

UNA MUJER = A WOMAN

UNA NOVIA = A GIRLFRIEND

Definite Article:

There is also a Definite Article that corresponds with the English 'THE.' It is always placed before the noun. The Definite Article has a masculine and feminine form, both singular and plural.

	Masculine	Feminine
Singular	EL (L')	LA (L')
Plural	LOS (L')	LAS (L')

*[L'] is used before nouns that start with a vowel

EL GATO = THE CAT

LOS GATOS = THE CATS

EL PERRO = THE DOG

LOS PERROS = THE DOGS

LA KRAVATA = THE NECKTIE

LAS KRAVATAS = THE NECKTIES

LA KASHA = THE BOX

LAS KASHAS = THE BOXES

EL LIVRO = THE BOOK

LOS LIVROS = THE BOOKS

LA KAZAS = THE HOUSE

LAS KAZAS = THE HOUSES

EL ASENTADOR = THE SEAT

L'ASENTADOR = THE SEAT

LOS ASENTADORES = THE SEATS

L'ASENTADORES = THE SEATS

EL KUCHIYO = THE KNIFE

LOS KUCHIYOS = THE KNIVES

EL PAIS = THE COUNTRY

LOS PAISES = THE COUNTRIES

LA FAMIYA = THE FAMILY

LAS FAMIYAS = THE FAMILIES

LA PARED = THE WALL

LAS PAREDES = THE WALLS

EL PERRO = THE DOG

LOS PERROS = THE DOGS

EL KOCHE = THE CAR

LOS KOCHES = THE CARS

LA MUJER = THE WOMAN

LAS MUJERES = THE WOMEN

IRREGULAR NOUNS:

EL AGUA = THE WATER

L'AGUA = THE WATER

LAS AGUAS = THE WATERS

L'AGUAS = THE WATERS

EL ARTE = THE ART

L'ARTE = THE ART

LAS ARTES = THE ARTS

L'ARTES = THE ARTS

EL MAPA = THE MAP

EL ALMA = THE SOUL

L'ALMA = THE SOUL

IV) The Adjective

Adjectives can be located before or after the nouns. The Adjective can only precede the noun when it is preceded by a Definite Article. Adjectives match the noun in gender, whether masculine or feminine, and number, whether singular or plural.

Adjectives:

GRANDE (Big)

DULSE (Sweet)

MUEVO (New)

FERMOZO (Beautiful)

BUENO (Good)

MALO (Bad, Evil)

CHIKO (Small)

KAYENTE (Hot)

YELADO (Cold)

GODRO (Fat)

FLAKO (Skinny)

PIKANTE (Spicy)

KONTENTE (Happy)

FELICHE (Happy)

EMPORTANTE (Important)

ENLOKESIDO (Crazy)

VIVO (Alive)

SUZIO (Dirty)

BOVO (Stupid)

LIMPIO (Clean)

KLARO (Clear)

MISERAVLE (Miserable)

OBEISENTE (Obedient)

ESKURO (Dark)

FEO (Ugly)

ALTO I FLAKO (Tall and Skinny)

*JUDEO-SPANISH IS HIGHLY GENDERED; EVEN MORE SO THAN REGULAR SPANISH

Ex.

GRANDE [m.] < **GRANDA** [f.]

DULSE [m.] < **DULSA** [f.]

KONTENTE [m.] < **KONTENTA** [f.]

KAYENTE [m.] < **KAYENTA** [f.]

PIKANTE [m.] < **PIKANTA** [f.]

FELICHE [m.] < **FELICHA** [f.]

EMPORTANTE [m.] < **EMPORTANTA** [f.]

*In regular Spanish these types of nouns have no particular gender and in their singular forms stay the same as the masculine forms shown above.

MUY (very…) This particle is added before the adjective and it gives emphasis to the adjective.

Example:

LA KOMIDA ES **MUY** DELISIOZA = The food is **very** delicious / tasty.

COMPARATIVES AND SUPERLATIVES:

Regular Comparatives:

RAPIDO = FAST   [KE = THAN]

MAS / MAZ RAPIDO = FASTER

FERMOZO = BEAUTIFUL

MAS / MAZ FERMOZO = MORE BEAUTIFUL

Regular Superlatives:

EL MAS / MAZ RAPIDO = FASTEST

EL MAS / MAZ FERMOZO = MOST BEAUTIFUL

Irregular Comparative:

BUENO = GOOD

MIJOR = BETTER

Irregular Superlative:

EL MIJOR = BEST

*NOTE: THERE ARE SEVERAL ADJECTIVES IN JUDEO-SPANISH THAT HAVE IRREGULAR COMPARATIVE AND SUPERLATIVE FORMS. THEY ARE THE SAME FORMS COMMON IN MODERN SPANISH.

Examples:

OMBRE **ENLOKESIDO** – CRAZY MAN

MUJER **FERMOZA** – BEAUTIFUL WOMAN

MANSEVO **FLAKO** – SKINNY KID

AZE TANTO **YELADO** – IT IS VERY COLD

LA KOMIDA ES **PIKANTE** – THE FOOD IS SPICY

EYA ES **MAZ FERMOZA KE** TU = SHE IS MORE

BEAUTIFUL THAN YOU

EYA TIENE LOS OJOS **MAZ FERMOZOS** = SHE HAS

THE MOST BEAUTIFUL EYES

EL ES **MIJOR KE** EL OTRO OMBRE = HE IS BETTER

THAN THE OTHER MAN

V)   This and That, Here and There

There are a couple ways to express 'This' and 'That' in the Judeo-Spanish Language:

THIS

ESTE / ESTA (masc. & fem.) = This

ESTOS / ESTAS (masc. pl & fem. pl) = These

Ex.

ESTE LUGAR ES FERMOZO = THIS PLACE IS BEAUTIFUL

ESTE ES MI AMIGO = THIS IS MY FRIEND

ESTE ES EL PERRO DE MI ERMANIKO = THIS IS MY BROTHER'S DOG

ESTA MUJER ME DIHO ESTE = THIS WOMAN TOLD ME IT

ESTOS OMBRES VAN AL LAVORO = THESE MEN ARE GOING TO WORK

ESTOS DJUGETES ESTAN ROTOS = THESE TOYS ARE BROKEN

THAT

AKEL / AKEYA (masc. & fem) = That

AKEYOS / AKEYAS (masc. pl & fem. pl) = Those

NOTE: ESE, ESA, ESOS, ESAS FORMS FOR 'THAT' WERE NOT PRESERVED IN JUDEO-SPANISH

Ex.

AKEYA MUJER ES FERMOZA = THAT WOMAN IS BEAUTIFUL

AKEYOS DÍAS AVEN IDO = THOSE DAYS HAVE GONE

AKEYAS MUJERES VAN AL SUPERMARKET = THOSE WOMEN ARE GOING TO THE SUPERMARKET

AKEYOS OMBRES VAN AL LAVORO = THOSE MEN ARE GOING TO WORK

Here and There:

AKI = HERE; HITHER

PARA AKI = HITHER

DE AKI = FROM HERE

VENTE PARA **AKI**! = COME HERE!

NOS KEDAMOS **AKI**! = LET'S STAY HERE!

AYI / AYA = THERE; THITHER

PARA AYI / PARA AYA = THITHER

DE AYI / AYA = FROM THERE

VETE PARA **AYA**! = GO THERE!

ME KEDO **AYI** = I AM STAYING THERE

Examples:

KE ES **ESTE**?

(What is that?)

ESTE ES MI PADRE

(This is my dad)

NO / NON KERO AZER **ESTE**

(I do not want to do this)

VENTE **AKI**!

(Come here!)

VENID **AKI**!

(Come here!)

VETE **AYI**!

(Go there!)

ID **AYA**!

(Go there!)

TRAELDO **AKI**!

(Bring it here!)

BIVO **AKI**

(I live here)

VI)   Interrogatives

Forming an Interrogative in the Judeo-Spanish Language can be done with either an Adverb or by changing the tone of voice while pronouncing the sentence.

The Interrogatives (Adverbs) in the Judeo-Spanish Language are:

ANDE? = Where? To where? Whither?

ANDE? = Where? Whereabouts?

DE ANDE? = From where? Whence?

KUANDO? = When?

KUANTO? = How much?

KOMO? = How?

KE? KUALO/A? = What? Which?

DE KE...? = About What?

PORKE? = Why?

KE TIPO DE...? = What kind of...?

KEN? = Who?

KON KEN? = With whom?

KON KUALO/A? = With what?

KUALO/A? = Which?

DE KEN? = From whom?

KE TIENE...? = Whose?

DONDE? = Whose? Of whom? Of which?

In order to create a question in the Spanish Language without an Adverb, the speaker will have to speak with a low to high tone as they speak the sentence.

TONE RISES FROM THE FRONT OF THE SENTENCE AND DECREASES TOWARDS THE END OF THE SENTENCE

AY ...? = IS THERE / ARE THERE...?

AY UN GATO EN LA KAZA = THERE IS A CAT IN THE HOUSE
AY UN GATO EN LA KAZA? = IS THERE A CAT IN THE HOUSE?

TIENES TU / **TENÉSH** VOZÓS...? = DO YOU HAVE...?

Example:

TIENES UN KALEM? = DO YOU HAVE A PENCIL?
TENÉSH VOZÓS UN KALEM? = DO YOU HAVE A PENCIL?
*THE VERB WILL ALWAYS BE SPOKEN IN A HIGHER TONE AND THE TONE DECREASES TOWARDS THE END OF THE SENTENCE

Examples:

ANDE ESTA TU KAZA? = Where is your home?

PORKE ME AYUDAS? = Why do you hate me?

KON KEN FUITES TU? = With whom did you go?

KUANTO KOSTA ESTE? = How much does it cost?

KOMO ESTASH? = How are you?

DE ANDE SOS TU? = Where are you from?

ANDE ESTASH? = Where are you?

VII)   Sentence Structure

The construction of the Judeo-Spanish phrase is as follows:

S-V-O (Subject -Verb -Object)

[most common when the Direct Object is a Noun]

or

S-O-V (Subject-Object-Verb)

[most common when Direct Object is a Pronoun]

All sentences will follow this order.

The following examples will be broken down piece by piece in order to show the reader a basic example of the word order for the Spanish Language:

(S-V-O)

EL OMBRE <u>BEZÓ</u> (*A*) *LA MUJER*

THE MAN <u>KISSED</u> *THE WOMAN*

EL OMBRE = THE MAN

LA MUJER = THE WOMAN

<u>BEZÓ</u> = KISSED (THE COMPLETIVE ASPECT OF THE VERB IS IMPLIED)

(S-O-V)

YO *TE* <u>AMO</u> = I LOVE YOU

YO = I (SUBJECT OF THE SENTENCE)

TE = YOU (DIRECT OBJECT)

<u>AMO</u> = I LOVE [1ST PERSON SING. PRESENT]

YO *LO* <u>IZI</u> = I DID IT

YO = I (SUBJECT OF THE SENTENCE)

LO = IT (DIRECT OBJECT)

<u>IZI</u> = DID/MADE [1ST PERSON SING. PRETERITE]

VIII) Verbs (Present, Past, Future, and Conditional)

There are several main tenses that can be expressed in the Judeo-Spanish Language: Present, Past, Imperfect, Future & Conditional. All verbs tend to have predictable conjugation depending on whether they have '-ar' or '-er' or '-ir' suffixes connected to the main verbal root.

Basic Copulas in Judeo-Espanyol:

Present Tense:

	-ar / -er,-ir	-ar / -er / -ir
1	-O	-AMOS / -EMOS / -IMOS
2	-AS / -ES	-ÁSH / -ÉSH / -ISH
3	-A / -E	-AN / -EN

Past Tense:

	-ar / -er,-ir	-ar / -er, -ir
1	-Í / I	-IMOS
2	-ATES / -ITES	-ATESH / -ITESH
3	-Ó / -IO	-ARON / -IERON

Imperfect Tense:

	-ar / -er,-ir	-ar / -er, -ir
1	-AVA / -IA	-ÁVAMOS / -IAMOS
2	-AVAS / -IAS	-ÁVASH / -IASH
3	-AVA / -IA	-AVAN / -IAN

Future Tense:

-ar / -er / -ir

1	-ARÉ / -ERE / -IRE
2	-ARÁS / -ERAS / -IRAS
3	-ARÁ / -ERA / -IRA
1	-AREMOS / -EREMOS / -IREMOS
2	-ARÉSH / -ERESH / -IRESH
3	-ARÁN / -ERAN / -IRAN

Conditional:

-ar / -er / -ir

1	-ARÍA / -ERIA / -IRIA
2	-ARÍAS / -ERIAS / -IRIAS
3	-ARÍA / -ERIA / -IRIA
1	-ARÍAMOS / -ERIAMOS / -IRIAMOS
2	-ARÍASH / -ERIASH / -IRIASH
3	-ARÍAN / -ERIAN / -IRIAN

Subjunctive:

	-ar / -er,-ir	-ar / -er, -ir
1	-O / -A	-EMOS / -AMOS
2	-ES / -AS	-ÉSH / -ASH
3	-E / -A	-EN / -AN

Imperfect Subjunctive:

	-ar / -er,-ir	-ar / -er, -ir
1	-ARA / -IERA	-ARAMOS / -IERAMOS
2	-ARAS / -IERAS	-ARASH / -IERASH
3	-ARA / -IERA	-ARAN / -IERAN

Perfect Tense:

      -ar / -er,-ir

1   AVO -ADO / -IDO

2   AVES -ADO / -IDO

3   AVE -ADO / -IDO

1   AVEMOS -ADO / -IDO

2   AVÉSH -ADO / -IDO

3   AVEN -ADO / -IDO

PRESENT TENSE:

Basic Verb: KANTAR = TO SING ('-AR' ROOT)

1	KANTO	KANTAMOS
2	KANTAS	KANTÁSH
3	KANTA	KANTAN

PAST TENSE:

Basic Verb: KANTAR = TO SING ('-AR' ROOT)

1	KANTÍ	KANTIMOS
2	KANTATES	KANTATESH
3	KANTÒ	KANTARON

IMPERFECT TENSE:

Basic Verb: KANTAR = TO SING ('-AR' ROOT)

1	KANTAVA	KANTAVAMOS
2	KANTAVAS	KANTAVASH
3	KANTAVA	KANTAVAN

FUTURE TENSE:

Basic Verb: KANTAR = TO SING ('-AR' ROOT)

1	KANTARÉ	KANTAREMOS
2	KANTARÁS	KANTARESH
3	KANTARÁ	KANTARÁN

CONDITIONAL:

Basic Verb: KANTAR = TO SING ('-AR' ROOT)

1	KANTARIA	KANTARIAMOS
2	KANTARIAS	KANTARIASH
3	KANTARIA	KANTARIAN

SUBJUNCTIVE:

Basic Verb: KANTAR = TO SING ('-AR' ROOT)

1	KANTO	KANTEMOS
2	KANTES	KANTÉSH
3	KANTE	KANTEN

IMPERFECT SUBJUNCTIVE:

Basic Verb: KANTAR = TO SING ('-AR' ROOT)

1   KANTARA   KANTARAMOS

2   KANTARAS   KANTARASH

3   KANTARA   KANTARAN

PERFECT TENSE:

Basic Verb: KANTAR = TO SING ('-AR' ROOT)

1   AVO KANTADO   AVEMOS KANTADO

2   AVES KANTADO   AVÉSH KANTADO

3   AVE KANTADO   AVEN KANTADO

PRESENT TENSE:

Basic Verb: KOMER = TO EAT ('-ER' ROOT)

1	KOMO	KOMEMOS
2	KOMES	KOMÉSH
3	KOME	KOMEN

PAST TENSE:

Basic Verb: KOMER = TO EAT ('-ER' ROOT)

1	KOMÍ	KOMIMOS
2	KOMITES	KOMITESH
3	KOMIO	KOMIERON

IMPERFECT TENSE:

Basic Verb: KOMER = TO EAT ('-ER' ROOT)

1	KOMIA	KOMIAMOS
2	KOMIAS	KOMIASH
3	KOMIA	KOMIAN

FUTURE TENSE:

Basic Verb: KOMER = TO EAT ('-ER' ROOT)

1	KOMERÉ	KOMEREMOS
2	KOMERÁS	KOMERESH
3	KOMERÁ	KOMERÁN

CONDITIONAL:

Basic Verb: KOMER = TO EAT ('-ER' ROOT)

1	KOMERIA	KOMERIAMOS
2	KOMERIAS	KOMERIASH
3	KOMERIA	KOMERIAN

SUBJUNCTIVE:

Basic Verb: KOMER = TO EAT ('-ER' ROOT)

1	KOMA	KOMAMOS
2	KOMAS	KOMASH
3	KOMA	KOMAN

IMPERFECT SUBJUNCTIVE:

Basic Verb: KOMER = TO EAT ('-ER' ROOT)

1   KOMIERA   KOMIERAMOS

2   KOMIERAS   KOMIERASH

3   KOMIERA   KOMIERAN

PERFECT TENSE:

Basic Verb: KOMER = TO EAT ('-ER' ROOT)

1   AVO KOMIDO   AVEMOS KOMIDO

2   AVES KOMIDO   AVÉSH KOMIDO

3   AVE KOMIDO   AVEN KOMIDO

PRESENT TENSE:

Basic Verb: BIVIR = TO LIVE ('-IR' ROOT)

1	BIVO	BIVIMOS
2	BIVES	BIVISH
3	BIVE	BIVEN

PAST TENSE:

Basic Verb: BIVIR = TO LIVE ('-IR' ROOT)

1	BIVI	BIVIMOS
2	BIVITES	BIVITESH
3	BIVIO	BIVIERON

IMPERFECT TENSE:

Basic Verb: BIVIR = TO LIVE ('-IR' ROOT)

1	BIVIA	BIVIAMOS
2	BIVIAS	BIVIASH
3	BIVIA	BIVIAN

FUTURE TENSE:

Basic Verb: BIVIR = TO LIVE ('-IR' ROOT)

1	BIVIRÉ	BIVIREMOS
2	BIVIRÁS	BIVIRÉSH
3	BIVIRÁ	BIVIRÁN

CONDITIONAL:

Basic Verb: BIVIR = TO LIVE ('-IR' ROOT)

1	BIVIRIA	BIVIRIAMOS
2	BIVIRIAS	BIVIRIASH
3	BIVIRIA	BIVIRIAN

SUBJUNCTIVE:

Basic Verb: BIVIR = TO LIVE ('-IR' ROOT)

1	BIVA	BIVAMOS
2	BIVAS	BIVASH
3	BIVA	BIVAN

IMPERFECT SUBJUNCTIVE:

Basic Verb: BIVIR = TO LIVE ('-IR' ROOT)

1   BIVIERA   BIVIERAMOS

2   BIVIERAS   BIVIERASH

3   BIVIERA   BIVIERAN

PERFECT TENSE:

Basic Verb: BIVIR = TO LIVE ('-IR' ROOT)

1   AVO BIVIDO   AVEMOS BIVIDO

2   AVES BIVIDO   AVÉSH BIVIDO

3   AVE BIVIDO   AVEN BIVIDO

PRESENT TENSE:

Basic Verb: ESKRIVIR = TO WRITE ('-IR' ROOT)

1	ESKRIVO	ESKRIVIMOS
2	ESKRIVES	ESKRIVISH
3	ESKRIVE	ESKRIVEN

PAST TENSE:

Basic Verb: ESKRIVIR = TO WRITE ('-IR' ROOT)

1	ESKRIVI	ESKRIVIMOS
2	ESKRIVITES	ESKRIVITESH
3	ESKRIVIO	ESKRIVIERON

PERFECT TENSE:

Basic Verb: ESKRIVIR = TO WRITE ('-IR' ROOT)

1	AVO ESKRITO	AVEMOS ESKRITO
2	AVES ESKRITO	AVÉSH ESKRITO
3	AVE ESKRITO	AVEN ESKRITO

PRESENT TENSE:

Basic Verb: IR = TO GO ('-IR' ROOT)

1	VO	VAMOS
2	VAS	VASH
3	VA	VAN

PAST TENSE:

Basic Verb: IR = TO GO ('-IR' ROOT)

1   FUI / HUI

2   FUITES / HUITES

3   FUE / HUE

1   FUIMOS / HUIMOS

2   FUITESH / HUITESH

3   FUERON / HUERON

IMPERFECT TENSE:

Basic Verb: IR = TO GO ('-IR' ROOT)

1	IVA	IVAMOS
2	IVAS	IVASH
3	IVA	IVAN

FUTURE TENSE:

Basic Verb: IR = TO GO ('-IR' ROOT)

1	IRÉ	IREMOS
2	IRÁS	IRESH
3	IRÁ	IRÁN

CONDITIONAL:

Basic Verb: IR = TO GO ('-IR' ROOT)

1	IRIA	IRIAMOS
2	IRIAS	IRIASH
3	IRIA	IRIAN

SUBJUNCTIVE:

Basic Verb: IR = TO GO ('-IR' ROOT)

1	VAYA	VAYAMOS
2	VAYAS	VAYASH
3	VAYA	VAYAN

IMPERFECT SUBJUNCTIVE:

Basic Verb: IR = TO GO ('-IR' ROOT)

1   FUERA / HUERA

2   FUERAS / HUERAS

3   FUERA / HUERA

1   FUERAMOS / HUERAMOS

2   FUERASH / HUERASH

3   FUERAN / HUERAN

PERFECT TENSE:

Basic Verb: IR = TO GO ('-IR' ROOT)

1	AVO IDO	AVEMOS IDO	
2	AVES IDO	AVÉSH IDO	
3	AVE IDO	AVEN IDO	

PRESENT TENSE:

Basic Verb: VENIR = TO COME ('-IR' ROOT)

1	VENGO	VENIMOS
2	VIENES	VENISH
3	VIENE	VIENEN

PAST TENSE:

Basic Verb: VENIR = TO COME ('-IR' ROOT)

1	VINI	VINIMOS
2	VINITES	VINITESH
3	VINO	VINIERON

IMPERFECT TENSE:

Basic Verb: VENIR = TO COME ('-IR' ROOT)

1	VENIA	VENIAMOS
2	VENIAS	VENIASH
3	VENIA	VENIAN

FUTURE TENSE:

Basic Verb: VENIR = TO COME ('-IR' ROOT)

1	VENDRÉ	VENDREMOS
2	VENDRÁS	VENDRÁSH
3	VENDRÁ	VENDRÁN

CONDITIONAL:

Basic Verb: VENIR = TO COME ('-IR' ROOT)

1	VENDRIA	VENDRIAMOS
2	VENDRIAS	VENDRIASH
3	VENDRIA	VENDRIAN

SUBJUNCTIVE:

Basic Verb: VENIR = TO COME ('-IR' ROOT)

1	VENGA	VENGAMOS
2	VENGAS	VENGASH
3	VENGA	VENGAN

IMPERFECT SUBJUNCTIVE:

Basic Verb: VENIR = TO COME ('-IR' ROOT)

1	VINIERA	VINIERAMOS
2	VINIERAS	VINIERASH
3	VINIERA	VINIERAN

PERFECT TENSE:

Basic Verb: VENIR = TO COME ('-IR' ROOT)

1	AVO VENIDO	AVEMOS VENIDO
2	AVES VENIDO	AVÉSH VENIDO
3	AVE VENIDO	AVEN VENIDO

PRESENT TENSE:

Basic Verb: TENER = TO HAVE ('-ER' ROOT)

1	TENGO	TENEMOS
2	TIENES	TENÉSH
3	TIENE	TIENES

PAST TENSE:

Basic Verb: TENER = TO HAVE ('-ER' ROOT)

1	TUVI	TUVIMOS
2	TUVITES	TUVITESH
3	TUVO	TUVIERON

FUTURE TENSE:

Basic Verb: TENER = TO HAVE ('-ER' ROOT)

1	TENDRÉ	TENDREMOS
2	TENDRÁS	TENDRÁSH
3	TENDRÁ	TENDRÁN

SUBJUNCTIVE:

Basic Verb: TENER = TO HAVE ('-ER' ROOT)

1	TENGA	TENGAMOS
2	TENGAS	TENGASH
3	TENGA	TENGAN

IMPERFECT SUBJUNCTIVE:

Basic Verb: TENER = TO HAVE ('-ER' ROOT)

1	TUVIERA	TUVIERAMOS
2	TUVIERAS	TUVIERASH
3	TUVIERA	TUVIERAN

PERFECT TENSE:

Basic Verb: TENER = TO HAVE ('-ER' ROOT)

1	AVO TENIDO	AVEMOS TENIDO
2	AVES TENIDO	AVÉSH TENIDO
3	AVE TENIDO	AVEN TENIDO

PRESENT TENSE:

Basic Verb: AZER = TO DO ('-ER' ROOT)

1	AGO	AZEMOS
2	AZES	AZESH
3	AZE	AZEN

PAST TENSE:

Basic Verb: AZER = TO DO ('-ER' ROOT)

1	IZI	IZIMOS
2	IZITES	IZITESH
3	IZO	IZIERON

FUTURE TENSE:

Basic Verb: AZER = TO DO ('-ER' ROOT)

1	ARÉ	AREMOS
2	ARÁS	ARÉSH
3	ARÁ	ARÁN

SUBJUNCTIVE:

Basic Verb: AZER = TO DO ('-ER' ROOT)

1	AGA	AGAMOS
2	AGAS	AGASH
3	AGA	AGAN

PERFECT TENSE:

Basic Verb: AZER = TO DO ('-ER' ROOT)

1	AVO ECHO	AVEMOS ECHO
2	AVES ECHO	AVÉSH ECHO
3	AVE ECHO	AVEN ECHO

PRESENT TENSE:

Basic Verb: SAVER = TO KNOW ('-ER' ROOT)

1	SE	SAVEMOS
2	SAVES	SAVÉSH
3	SAVE	SAVEN

PAST TENSE

Basic Verb: SAVER = TO KNOW ('-ER' ROOT)

1	SUPI	SUPIMOS
2	SUPITES	SUPITESH
3	SUPO	SUPIERON

FUTURE TENSE

Basic Verb: SAVER = TO KNOW ('-ER' ROOT)

1	SAVRÉ	SAVREMOS
2	SAVRÁS	SAVRÉSH
3	SAVRÁ	SAVRÁN

SUBJUNCTIVE

Basic Verb: SAVER = TO KNOW ('-ER' ROOT)

1	SEPA	SEPAMOS
2	SEPAS	SEPASH
3	SEPA	SEPAN

PERFECT TENSE

Basic Verb: SAVER = TO KNOW ('-ER' ROOT)

1	AVO SAVIDO	AVEMOS SAVIDO
2	AVES SAVIDO	AVÉSH SAVIDO
3	AVE SAVIDO	AVEN SAVIDO

PRESENT TENSE:

Basic Verb: KONOSER = TO KNOW ('-ER' ROOT)

1	KONOSKO	KONOSEMOS
2	KONOSES	KONOSÉSH
3	KONOSE	KONOSEN

PAST TENSE:

Basic Verb: KONOSER = TO KNOW ('-ER' ROOT)

1	KONOSÍ	KONOSIMOS
2	KONOSITES	KONOSITESH
3	KONOSIO	KONOSIERON

SUBJUNCTIVE:

Basic Verb: KONOSER = TO KNOW ('-ER' ROOT)

1	KONOSKA	KONOSKAMOS
2	KONOSKAS	KONOSKASH
3	KONOSKA	KONOSKAN

PRESENT TENSE:

Basic Verb: DAR = TO GIVE ('-AR' ROOT)

1	DO	DAMOS
2	DAS	DÁSH
3	DA	DAN

PAST TENSE:

Basic Verb: DAR = TO GIVE ('-AR' ROOT)

1	DI	DIMOS
2	DITES	DITESH
3	DIO	DIERON

IMPERFECT TENSE:

Basic Verb: DAR = TO GIVE ('-AR' ROOT)

1	DAVA	DAVAMOS
2	DAVAS	DAVÁSH
3	DAVA	DAVAN

FUTURE TENSE:

Basic Verb:　DAR = TO GIVE ('-AR' ROOT)

1	DARÉ	DAREMOS
2	DARÁS	DARÉSH
3	DARÁ	DARÁN

PERFECT TENSE:

Basic Verb:　DAR = TO GIVE ('-AR' ROOT)

1	AVO DADO	AVEMOS DADO
2	AVES DADO	AVÉSH DADO
3	AVE DADO	AVEN DADO

PRESENT TENSE:

Basic Verb: DEZIR = TO SAY ('-IR' ROOT)

1	DIGO	DIZIMOS
2	DIZES	DIZISH
3	DIZE	DIZEN

PAST TENSE:

Basic Verb: DEZIR = TO SAY ('-IR' ROOT)

1	DIHI	DIHIMOS
2	DIHITES	DIHITESH
3	DIHO	DIHIERON

IMPERFECT TENSE:

Basic Verb: DEZIR = TO SAY ('-IR' ROOT)

1	DEZIA	DEZIAMOS
2	DEZIAS	DEZIASH
3	DEZIA	DEZIAN

FUTURE TENSE:

Basic Verb: DEZIR = TO SAY ('-IR' ROOT)

1	DIRÉ	DIREMOS
2	DIRÁS	DIRESH
3	DIRÁ	DIRÁN

SUBJUNCTIVE TENSE:

Basic Verb: DEZIR = TO SAY ('-IR' ROOT)

1	DIGA	DIGAMOS
2	DIGAS	DIGASH
3	DIGA	DIGAN

PERFECT TENSE:

Basic Verb: DEZIR = TO SAY ('-IR' ROOT)

1	AVO DICHO	AVEMOS DICHO
2	AVES DICHO	AVÉSH DICHO
3	AVE DICHO	AVEN DICHO

PRESENT TENSE:

Basic Verb: KONTAR = TO TELL ('-AR' ROOT)

1	KONTO	KONTAMOS
2	KONTAS	KONTASH
3	KONTA	KONTAN

PRESENT TENSE:

Basic Verb: PENSAR = TO THINK ('-AR' ROOT)

1	PENSO	PENSAMOS
2	PENSAS	PENSASH
3	PENSA	PENSAN

PRESENT TENSE:

Basic Verb: VER = TO SEE (IRREG. 'ER' ROOT)

1	VEO	VEMOS
2	VES	VESH
3	VE	VEN

PAST TENSE:

Basic Verb: VER = TO SEE (IRREG. 'ER' ROOT)

1	VÍ	VIMOS
2	VITES	VITESH
3	VIO	VIERON

PERFECT TENSE:

Basic Verb: VER = TO SEE (IRREG. 'ER' ROOT)

1	AVO VISTO	AVEMOS VISTO
2	AVES VISTO	AVÉSH VISTO
3	AVE VISTO	AVEN VISTO

PRESENT TENSE:

Basic Verb: UZAR = TO USE ('-AR' ROOT)

1	UZO	UZAMOS
2	UZAS	UZASH
3	UZA	UZAN

PRESENT TENSE:

Basic Verb: OYIR = TO HEAR ('-IR' ROOT)

1	OYGO	OYIMOS
2	OYES	OYISH
3	OYE	OYEN

PRESENT TENSE:

Basic Verb: MURIR = TO DIE ('-IR' ROOT)

1	MURO	MURIMOS
2	MURES	MURISH
3	MURE	MUREN

PRESENT TENSE:

Basic Verb: PUEDER   =   TO   BE   ABLE   TO
('-ER' ROOT)

1	PUEDO	PUEDEMOS
2	PUEDES	PUEDESH
3	PUEDE	PUEDEN

PRESENT TENSE:

Basic Verb: VALER = TO BE WORTH ('-ER' ROOT)

1	VALGO	VALEMOS
2	VALES	VALESH
3	VALE	VALEN

PRESENT TENSE:

Basic Verb: AVLAR / FAVLAR =

TO SPEAK ('-AR' ROOT)

1	AVLO / FAVLO	AVLAMOS / FAVLAMOS
2	AVLAS / FAVLAS	AVLASH / FAVLASH
3	AVLA / FAVLA	AVLAN / FAVLAN

112

PRESENT TENSE:

Basic Verb: BEZAR = TO KISS ('-AR' ROOT)

1	BEZO	BEZAMOS
2	BEZAS	BEZASH
3	BEZA	BEZAN

PRESENT TENSE:

Basic Verb: ENTENDER =

TO UNDERSTAND ('-ER' ROOT)

1   ENTENDO / ENTIENDO

2   ENTENDES / ENTIENDES

3   ENTENDE / ENTIENDE

1   ENTENDEMOS

2   ENTENDESH

3   ENTENDEN / ENTIENDEN

*Many verbs have an 'e' < 'ie' conjugation and can be either or in Judeo-Spanish as can be seen above.

PRESENT TENSE:

Basic Verb: VIAJAR = TO TRAVEL ('-AR' ROOT)

1	VIAJO	VIAJAMOS
2	VIAJAS	VIAJASH
3	VIAJA	VIAJAN

*Remember that 'J' has the sound of 's' in the word 'leisure' and thus, it takes on a 'zh' sound value

PERFECT TENSE:

Basic Verb: VIAJAR = TO TRAVEL ('-AR' ROOT)

1	AVO VIAJADO	AVEMOS VIAJADO
2	AVES VIAJADO	AVESH VIAJADO
3	AVE VIAJADO	AVEN VIAJADO

*Remember that 'J' has the sound of 's' in the word 'leisure' and thus, it takes on a 'zh' sound value

114

PRESENT TENSE:

Basic Verb: KERER = TO WANT ('-ER' ROOT)

1	KERO / KIERO	KEREMOS
2	KERES / KIERES	KERESH
3	KERE / KIERE	KEREN / KIEREN

PAST TENSE:

Basic Verb: KERER = TO WANT ('-ER' ROOT)

1	KIZI	KIZIMOS
2	KIZITES	KIZITESH
3	KIZO	KIZIERON

FUTURE TENSE:

Basic Verb: KERER = TO WANT ('-ER' ROOT)

1	KERRÉ	KERREMOS
2	KERRÁS	KERRÉSH
3	KERRÁ	KERRÁN

PRESENT TENSE:

Basic Verb: SER / ESTAR = TO BE

1	SE / ESTO	SEMOS / ESTAMOS
2	SOS / ESTAS	SOSH / ESTASH
3	ES / ESTA	SON / ESTAN

PAST TENSE:

Basic Verb: SER / ESTAR = TO BE

1	FUI / HUI	FUIMOS / HUIMOS
	ESTUVE	ESTUVIMOS
2	FUITES / HUITES	FUITESH / HUITESH
	ESTUVITES	ESTUVITESH
3	FUE / HUE	FUERON / HUERON
	ESTUVO	ESTUVIERON

FUTURE TENSE:

Basic Verb: SER / ESTAR = TO BE

1	SERÉ / ESTARÉ	SEREMOS / ESTAREMOS
2	SERÁS / ESTARÁS	SERÉSH / ESTARÉSH
3	SERÁ / ESTARÁ	SERÁN / ESTARÁN

PRESENT TENSE:

Basic Verb: AVER = TO HAVE ('-ER' ROOT)

1	AVO	AVEMOS
2	AVES	AVÉSH
3	AVE	AVEN

PAST TENSE:

Basic Verb: AVER = TO HAVE ('-ER' ROOT)

1	UVI	UVIMOS
2	UVITES	UVITESH
3	UVO	UVIERON

IMPERFECT TENSE:

Basic Verb: AVER = TO HAVE ('-ER' ROOT)

1	AVIA	AVIAMOS
2	AVIAS	AVIASH
3	AVIA	AVIAN

FUTURE TENSE:

Basic Verb: AVER = TO HAVE ('-ER' ROOT)

1	AVRÉ	AVREMOS
2	AVRÁS	AVRÉSH
3	AVRÁ	AVRÁN

CONDITIONAL:

Basic Verb: AVER = TO HAVE ('-ER' ROOT)

1	AVRÍA	AVRÍAMOS
2	AVRÍAS	AVRÍASH
3	AVRÍA	AVRÍAN

SUBJUNCTIVE TENSE:

Basic Verb: AVER = TO HAVE ('-ER' ROOT)

1	AYA	AYAMOS
2	AYAS	AYÁSH
3	AYA	AYAN

FUTURE #2:

Another way to create a simpler Future tense is by using the verb 'IR' [to go] + A [to] + INFINITIVE

IR A = GOING TO...

1   VO A   VAMOS A

2   VAS A   VASH A

3   VA A   VAN A

Ex.

VASH A NESESITAR UN KALEM = YOU WILL NEED A PENCIL

VO A IR A MI KAZA = I WILL GO HOME

VAMOS A AZERLO = WE WILL DO IT

VAS A TENER UN DOLOR DE KABESA = YOU WILL HAVE A HEADACHE

OTHER SPECIAL VERBAL CONSTRUCTIONS:

PERIPHRASTIC CONSTRUCTIONS –

ESTAR ...-NDO [PROGRESSIVE]

1	ESTO	ESTAMOS
2	ESTAS	ESTASH
3	ESTA	ESTAN

-AR < -ANDO = AVLANDO

-ER / -IR < -IENDO = PARTIENDO

Ex.

ESTO AZIE**NDO**LO = I AM DOING IT

ESTASH YE**NDO** = YOU ARE GOING

ESTAMOS AVLA**NDO** = WE ARE SPEAKING

ESTAS PARTIE**NDO** = YOU ARE LEAVING

VENIR DE [RECENTLY COMPLETED ACTION]

1	VENGO	VENIMOS
2	VENES / VIENES	VENISH
3	VENE / VIENE	VENEN / VIENEN

Ex.

VENGO DE AZERLO = I JUST DID IT

VENISH DE AVLAR = YOU JUST SPOKE

VENIMOS DE PARTIR = WE JUST LEFT

VENES DE AYUDARME = YOU JUST HELPED ME

TORNAR I [REPEATED ACTION]

1	TORNO	TORNAMOS
2	TORNAS	TORNASH
3	TORNA	TORNAN

Ex.

GRASIAS PARA **TORNAR I** VERME = THANK YOU FOR RETURNING TO SEE ME

VOY A **TORNAR I** AZERLO = I WILL DO IT AGAIN

EL VINO I DOSPUES EL **TORNÓ I** SALIR = HE CAME AND AFTERWARDS HE LEFT AGAIN

IX)   Negation

Negation of the Verbs:

In the Spanish Language, Negation is quite simple.

NO / **NON** (NO; NOT)

*THE NEGATIVE PARTICLE IS ALWAYS PLACED AFTER THE SUBJECT PRONOUN. IF THE SENTENCE LACKS A SUBJECT PRONOUN, THE PARTICLE IS ALWAYS PLACED BEFORE THE INITIAL VERB OR BEFORE ANY DIRECT OR INDIRECT OBJECTS IN THE PHRASE.

YO **NO** TE KERO AYUDAR = I **DO NOT** WANT TO HELP YOU

NO ME LO DITES = YOU **DID NOT** GIVE IT TO ME

NO LO ARÁS / **NO** VAS A AZERLO = YOU WILL **NOT** DO IT

X)   Commands [Imperatives]

Judeo-Spanish Imperatives have several key forms that are used across the board. All Imperative forms have a basic, polite and a plural form. There is also an Inclusive Imperative form in order to express 'let's…!'

A) THERE ARE FOUR FORMS OF THE STANDARD IMPERATIVE: BASIC [2ND PERSON SING], POLITE [3RD PERSON SING. SUBJ. PRESENT] & PLURAL [2ND PERSON PLURAL] AND [3RD PERSON PLURAL SUBJ. PRESENT]

B) THE INCLUSIVE FORM USES THE 1ST PERSON PLURAL SUBJ. PRESENT FORM.

C) THERE ARE SEVERAL VERBS THAT HAVE IRREGULAR IMPERATIVE VERB FORMS

-AR VERBS

1) MANDA! MANDE! = SEND! [SING.]

2) MANDAD! MANDEN! = SEND! [PL.]

3) VAMOS A MANDAR! MANDEMOS! = LET'S SEND! [INCLUSIVE]

-ER VERBS

1) KOME! KOMA! = EAT! [SING.]

2) KOMED! KOMAN! = EAT! [PL.]

3) VAMOS A KOMER! KOMAMOS! = LET'S EAT!

-IR VERBS

1) BIVE! BIVA! = LIVE! [SING.]

2) BIVID! BIVAN! = LIVE! [PL.]

3) ¡VAMOS A BIVIR! BIVAMOS! = LET'S LIVE!

IRREGULAR:

1) VETE! VAYASE! = GO! [SING.]

2) ID! VAYANSE! = GO! [PL.]

3) VAMOS! VAMONOS! VAYAMOS! = LET'S GO! [INCLUSIVE]

1) AZ! AGA! = DO! [SING.]

2) AZED! AGAN! = DO! [PL.]

3) AGAMOS! = LET'S DO! [INCLUSIVE]

*FOR THE INCLUSIVE IMPERATIVE VERBS USE:

VAMOS A… + [INFINITIVE]! = LET'S…

OR

THE 1ST PERSON PLURAL SUBJUNCTIVE PRESENT FORM:

AVLAR / FAVLAR [INFINITIVE] = TO SPEAK

AVLAMOS / FAVLAMOS [PRESENT] WE SPEAK < **AVLEMOS / FAVLEMOS** [SUBJ. PRESENT] =

MAY WE SPEAK! LET'S SPEAK!

*WITH SOME VERBS, THE IMPERATIVE CAN HAVE A REFLEXIVE PARTICLE '-NOS' ATTACHED TO ADD EMPHASIS, WHEN THE 1ST PERSON PLURAL PRESENT TENSE FORM IS USED.

'VAMONOS!' = VAMOS! – (S) + -NOS

SPECIAL CIRCUMSTANCES:

AZLO! / AGALO!

AZELDO / AGANLO! = DO IT! [IRREG.]

NOTE: VERBS IN THE 2ND PERS. PLURAL CAN BE BLENDED WITH THE 3RD PERS. DIRECT OBJECT:

Ex.

KOMED! + LO(S) / LA(S) =

KOMELDO! / KOMELDA! = EAT IT!

KOMELDOS! / KOMELDAS! = EAT THEM!

TRAED! + LO(S) / LA(S) =

TRAELDO! / TRAELDA! = BRING IT!

TRAELDOS! / TRAELDAS! = BRING THEM!

AZED! + LO(S) / LA(S) =

AZELDO! / AZELDA! = DO IT!

AZELDOS! / AZELDAS! = DO THEM!

OTHER IMPERATIVES:

SERRA! / SERRE! = CLOSE!

SERRAD! SERREN! = CLOSE!

SERREMOS! = LET'S CLOSE!

AVRE! / AVRA! = OPEN!

AVRID! / AVRAN! = OPEN!

AVRAMOS! = LET'S OPEN!

PERDONA! / PERDONE! = FORGIVE!

PERDONAD! / PERDONEN! = FORGIVE!

PERDONEMOS! = LET'S FORGIVE!

AYUDA! / AYUDE! = HELP!

AYUDAD! / AYUDEN! = HELP!

AYUDEMOS! = LET'S HELP!

*ALL GRAMMATICAL RULES APPLY WHEN CONSTRUCTING PHRASES WITH IMPERATIVES.

AYUDAME! / AYUDEME! = HELP ME!

AYUDADME! / AYUDENME! = HELP ME!

AVRE / **AVRA** LA PUERTA! = OPEN THE DOOR!

AVRID / **AVRAN** LA PUERTA! = OPEN THE DOOR!

SERRA / **SERRE** LA VENTANA! = CLOSE THE WINDOW!

SERRAD / **SERREN** LA VENTANA! = CLOSE THE WINDOW!

TRAELDO KON TI KUANDO VIENES! = BRING IT WITH YOU WHEN YOU COME!

XI)   Commands with negation

In order to create a Negative Imperative the speaker uses the standard Negative Particle 'NO' or 'NON' and the 2nd person singular and plural Subjunctive Present and the 3rd person singular Subjunctive Present in order to create a polite form.

CONSTRUCTION OF THE NEGATIVE COMMAND:

NO / NON (NEGATIVE PARTICLE) + (DIRECT OBJECT OR REFLEXIVE) *OPTIONAL IN SOME CASES* + 2ND PERSON SUBJUNCTIVE PRESENT SINGULAR OR PLURAL AND 3RD PERSON SINGULAR SUBJUNCTIVE PRESENT FOR POLITE FORM

NO / NON LO AGAS! = DON'T DO IT!
NO / NON LO AGA! = DON'T DO IT! [POLITE]
NO / NON LO AGAN! = DON'T DO IT! [PLURAL]
NO / NON TE VAYAS! = DON'T GO!
NO / NON SE VAYA! = DON'T GO! [POLITE]
NO / NON SE VAYAN! = DON'T GO! [PLURAL]
NO / NON SALGAS! = DON'T LEAVE!
NO / NON SALGA! = DON'T LEAVE! [POLITE]
NO / NON SALGAN! = DON'T LEAVE! [PLURAL]

NO / NON ME TOKES! = DON'T TOUCH ME!
NO / NON ME TOKE! = DON'T TOUCH ME! [POLITE]

NO / NON ME TOKEN! = DON'T TOUCH ME! [PLURAL]

NO / NON AVLES! = DON'T SPEAK!

NO / NON AVLE! = DON'T SPEAK! [POLITE]

NO / NON AVLEN! = DON'T SPEAK! [PLURAL]

XII)   To want to, to need to & to be able to

The following section will cover verb forms and constructions for 'I want to…, I need to… & I can / am able to…' in the Judeo-Spanish Language.

TO WANT TO…

PRESENT TENSE

<u>QUERER (TO WANT) [E] OR [E < IE]</u>

1   KERO / KIERO   KEREMOS

2   KERES / KIERES   KERESH

3   KERE / KIERE   KEREN / KIEREN

Ex.

KERO IR = I WANT TO GO

KERES / KIERES IR = YOU WANT TO GO

KERO / KIERO VENIR = I WANT TO COME

EL KERE VENIR = HE WANTS TO COME

KEREMOS KOMER = WE WANT TO EAT

KERO SALIR = I WANT TO LEAVE

KERO FUMAR UN SIGARO = I WANT TO SMOKE

KERES / KIERES DAR = YOU WANT TO GIVE

IMPERFECT, PRETERITE & CONDITIONAL:

IMPERFECT TENSE [IN THE PROCESS]:

1	KERÍA	KERÍAMOS
2	KERÍAS	KERÍAN
3	KERÍA	KERÍAN

PRETERITE TENSE [COMPLETIVE]:

1	KIZI	KIZIMOS
2	KIZITES	KIZITESH
3	KIZO	KIZIERON

CONDITIONAL:

1	KERRÍA	KERRÍAMOS
2	KERRÍAS	KERRÍASH
3	KERRÍA	KERRÍAN

FUTURE, SUBJ. PRESENT & SUBJ. PAST:

FUTURE:

1	KERRÉ	KERREMOS
2	KERRÁS	KERRÉSH
3	KERRÁ	KERRÁN

SUBJUNCTIVE PRESENT:

1	KERA / KIERA	KERAMOS / KIERAMOS
2	KERAS / KIERAS	KERASH / KIERASH
3	KERA / KIERA	KERAN / KIERAN

IMPERFECT SUBJUNCTIVE:

1	KIZIERA	KIZIERAMOS
2	KIZIERAS	KIZIERASH
3	KIZIERA	KIZIERAN

Ex.

YO **KERÍA** IR = I WANTED TO GO

MOSOTROS **KIZIMOS** KOMER = WE WANTED TO EAT

MOSOTROS **KERÍAMOS** IR = WE WANTED TO GO

KERO KE ME **KERAS** = I WANT YOU TO WANT ME

KIERO KE ME **KIERAS** = I WANT YOU TO WANT ME

KERRÉ IR AL SUPERMARKET = I WILL WANT TO GO TO THE SUPERMARKET

KERRÍA AZERLO = I WOULD WANT TO DO IT

TO NEED TO, OUGHT TO & TO HAVE TO:

PRESENT TENSE

I)   NESESITAR (TO NEED TO)

II)   DEVER (OUGHT TO / HAVE TO)

III)   TENER KE... (TO HAVE TO...)

PRESENT TENSE: NEED TO

1	NESESITO	NESESITAMOS
2	NESESITAS	NESESITASH
3	NESESITA	NESESITAN

PRESENT TENSE: OUGHT TO / HAVE TO

1	DEVO	DEVEMOS
2	DEVES	DEVESH
3	DEVE	DEVEN

PRESENT TENSE: HAVE TO

1   TENGO KE   TENEMOS KE

2   TENES / TIENES KE   TENESH KE

3   TENE / TIENE KE   TENEN / TIENEN KE

Ex.

NESESITO IR = I NEED TO GO

DEVO IR = I OUGHT TO GO

TENGO KE IR = I HAVE TO GO

NESESITO KOMER = I NEED TO EAT

DEVO KOMER = I OUGHT TO EAT

TENGO KE KOMER = I HAVE TO EAT

NESESITAS DURMIR = YOU NEED TO SLEEP

DEVES DURMIR = YOU OUGHT TO SLEEP

IMPERFECT & PRETERITE OF 'NESESITAR':

*IMPERFECTIVE [IN THE PROCESS]

1	NESESITAVA	NESESITAVAMOS
2	NESESITAVAS	NESESITAVASH
3	NESESITAVA	NESESITAVAN

PRETERITE [COMPLETIVE]

1	NESESITÍ	NESESITIMOS
2	NESESITATES	NESESITATESH
3	NESESITÓ	NESESITARON

Ex.

NESESITAVA IR = I NEEDED TO GO

NESESITÍ IR = I NEEDED TO GO

NESESITAVAS DURMIR = YOU NEEDED TO SLEEP

NESESITATES DURMIR = YOU NEEDED TO SLEEP

MOZOTROS **NESESITAVAMOS** KOMER =

WE NEEDED TO EAT

MOZOTROS **NESESITIMOS** KOMER =

WE NEEDEDTO EAT

I CAN / AM ABLE TO...

IN ORDER TO EXPRESS 'I CAN / AM ABLE TO...'

VERB: **PUEDER** = TO BE ABLE TO

YO **PUEDO** IR = I CAN GO

MOZOTROS **PUEDEMOS** KOMER = WE CAN EAT

NEGATION IS EXPRESSED WITH 'NO'

YO PUEDO... = I CAN...

*YO NO / NON PUEDO = I CANNOT...

PRESENT TENSE: PUEDER

1	PUEDO	PUEDEMOS
2	PUEDES	PUEDESH
3	PUEDE	PUEDEN

IMPERFECTIVE, PRETERITE & CONDITIONAL:

IMPERFECTIVE [STILL IN THE PROCESS]:

1	PUEDÍA	PUEDÍAMOS
2	PUEDÍAS	PUEDÍASH
3	PUEDÍA	PUEDÍAN

PRETERITE [COMPLETIVE]:

1	PUDI / PUEDI	PUDIMOS / PUEDIMOS
2	PUDITES	PUDITESH
	PUEDITES	PUEDITESH
3	PUDO / PUEDIO	PUDIERON / PUEDIERON

CONDITIONAL:

1	PUEDRÍA	PUEDRÍAMOS
2	PUEDRÍAS	PUEDRÍASH
3	PUEDRÍA	PUEDRÍAN

FUTURE #1:

1	PUEDRÉ	PUEDREMOS
2	PUEDRÁS	PUEDRÉSH
3	PUEDRÁ	PUEDRÁN

FUTURE #2: IR A... [MOST COMMON]

1	VO A PUEDER	VAMOS A PUEDER
2	VAS A PUEDER	VASH A PUEDER
3	VA A PUEDER	VAN A PUEDER

PERFECT, SUBJ. PRESENT & IMPRF. SUBJ. TENSES:

PERFECT:

1	AVO PUEDIDO	AVEMOS PUEDIDO
2	AVES PUEDIDO	AVÉSH PUEDIDO
3	AVE PUEDIDO	AVEN PUEDIDO

SUBJUNCTIVE PRESENT:

1	PUEDA	PUEDAMOS
2	PUEDAS	PUEDASH
3	PUEDA	PUEDAN

IMPERFECT SUBJUNCTIVE:

1	PUDIERA	PUDIERAMOS
	PUEDIERA	PUEDIERAMOS
2	PUDIERAS	PUDIERASH
	PUEDIERAS	PUEDIERASH
3	PUDIERA	PUDIERAN
	PUEDIERA	PUEDIERAN

NEGATION IS EXPRESSED THE SAME AS ALL STANDARD VERBS:

IMPERFECTIVE:

YO NO PUEDÍA... = I COULD NOT / WAS NOT ABLE TO... [STILL IN THE PROCESS]

PRETERITE:

YO NO PUDI / PUEDI... = I COULD NOT / WAS NOT ABLE TO...[COMPLETIVE]

CONDITIONAL:

YO NO PUEDRÍA… = I COULD NOT; WOULD NOT BE ABLE [CONDITIONAL]; WOULD BE ABLE TO…

Ex.

NO LO **PUDI / PUEDI** AZER = I COULD NOT DO IT

YO LO **PUEDRÍA** AZER = I COULD DO IT

YO **PUEDRÍA** IRME = I WOULD BE ABLE TO GO

TU **PUEDRÍAS** IR = YOU COULD GO

PUEDRÍAS TU AYUDARME? = COULD YOU HELP ME?

MOZOTROS **PUEDRÍAMOS** PARTIR = WE COULD LEAVE

NO **PUDIMOS / PUEDIMOS** PARTIR = WE COULD NOT LEAVE

XIII)   To have and to not have

In order to express, 'to have' and 'to not have' there is one verb that can be used to do so:

The basic structure of such a sentence would utilize the verb 'TENER' which means 'to have'

TENER (TO HAVE) + NOUN

TENGO UN KALEM = I HAVE A PENCIL

TENGO = I HAVE [1ST PERSON SING.]

UN KALEM = A PENCIL

TENER = TO HAVE [PRESENT TENSE]

1	TENGO	TENEMOS
2	TENES / TIENES	TENÉSH
3	TENE / TIENE	TENEN / TIENEN

TENGO UN ERMANIKO = I HAVE A BROTHER

TENGO UN GATO = I HAVE A CAT

TU TIENES / TENES UN PADRE = YOU HAVE A FATHER

TENÉSH UN PADRE? = DO YOU HAVE A FATHER?

*RAISED TONE OF VOICE WITH QUESTIONS THAT RISES FROM BEGINNING AND DECLINES TOWARD THE END OF A SENTENCE:

TIENES UN GATO? = DO YOU HAVE A CAT?

TENÉSH UN GATO? = DO YOU HAVE A CAT?

TIENES UN KALEM? = DO YOU HAVE A PENCIL?

TENÉSH UN KALEM? = DO YOU HAVE A PENCIL?

HAY UN KALEM? = IS THERE A PENCIL?

NEGATION:

NEGATION OF THE VERB 'TENER' IS EXPRESSED WITH THE SAME VERB, ONLY WITH THE NEGATIVE PARTICLE 'NO / NON':

NO / NON = NO

NO / NON + TENER [ANY TENSE]

Also, one should bear in mind that Judeo-Spanish is a double negative language just like Spanish. Therefore, to say 'not any' to go along with the initial negative particle; a special particle is used 'DINGUNO(S) / DINGUNA(S)' and these forms must match the noun being modified in gender and number.

Ex.

NO TENGO **DINGUNO** KALEM = I DON'T HAVE A
PENCIL

NO TENGO **DINGUNO** KALEM = I DON'T HAVE A
PENCIL

NON TENGO **DINGUNA** ESPOZA = I DON'T HAVE A
WIFE

NON TENGO **DINGUNA** ESPOSA = I DON'T HAVE A
WIFE

NON TENGO **DINGUNOS** AMIGOS = I DON'T HAVE
ANY FRIENDS

NON TENGO **DINGUNAS** AMIGAS = I DON'T HAVE
ANY FRIENDS

PAST TENSE (IMPERFECTIVE & PRETERITE):

THE PAST TENSE CAN BE EXPRESSED IN TWO WAYS:

THE IMPERFECTIVE: YO TENÍA (I HAD; WAS HAVING)

[LIT. I HAD IN THE PAST, BUT I DON'T RIGHT NOW]

THE PRETERITE: YO TUVI (I HAD)

[LIT. I HAD IN THE PAST AND I STILL DO NOT HAVE]

Ex.

TENÍA / TUVI UN KALEM = I HAD A PENCIL

NO TENÍA / TUVI DINGUNO KALEM = I DID NOT HAVE A PENCIL

NO TENÍAMOS / TUVIMOS DINGUNO GATO = WE DID NOT HAVE A CAT

TENER = TO HAVE [IMPERFECTIVE]

1	TENÍA	TENÍAMOS
2	TENÍAS	TENÍAN
3	TENÍA	TENÍAN

TENER = TO HAVE [PRETERITE]

1	TUVI	TUVIMOS
2	TUVITES	TUVITESH
3	TUVO	TUVIERON

TENER = TO HAVE [PERFECT] AVER + TENIDO

1	AVO TENIDO	AVEMOS TENIDO
2	AVES TENIDO	AVÉSH TENIDO
3	AVE TENIDO	AVEN TENIDO

XIV) Conjunctions

In order express a conjunction in the Guatemalan Spanish Language, one will have to utilize the basic conjunction 'KE' [THAT], and in some cases 'LO KE' is used and implies the meaning 'THAT WHICH'.

KERO **KE** ME AYUDES =

(I WANT **THAT** YOU HELP ME)

KERES **KE** YO LO AGA =

(YOU WANT **THAT** I DO THIS)

KERO **KE** TU LO AZES =

(I WANT **THAT** YOU DO THIS)

KERO **LO KE** KERAS =

(I WANT **WHAT** YOU WANT)

KERO **LO KE** TIENE EL

(I WANT WHAT HE HAS)

*AS WELL, CONJUNCTIONS SUCH AS 'KUANDO'
[WHEN] AND 'MA' [BUT] CAN BE USED.

MA = BUT (used in general)

*SINO = BUT (used when the first half of the sentence is negative)

Ex.

KERO SAVER KUANDO EL PARTE =
I WANT TO KNOW WHEN HE LEAVES
EYA KERE AYUDAR, MA EYA NON PUEDE =
SHE WANTS TO HELP BUT SHE CAN'T
EYA NON KERE AYUDAR, SINO EYA PUEDE =
SHE DOES NOT WANT TO HELP, BUT SHE CAN

Part II: Basic and Useful Vocabulary

English – Judeo-Spanish Dictionary

A

A Little = UN POKO

A, An (f.) = UNA

A, An (m.) = UNO

Ability = KAPACHEDAD

Abjection = BASHEZA

Able = KAPACHI

About = ENDRIVA

About = ENRIVA

About = SOVRE

Abraham = AVRAHAM

Absolute = ABSOLUTO

Acacia = AKASIA

Accident = AKSIDENTE

Account = KUENTA

Act = AKTO

Action = AKSION

Actor = AKTOR

Actress = AKTRISA

Address = ADRESO

Address = DIREKSION

Adjective = AJEKTIVO

Admiration = ADMIRASION

Adolescence = ADOLESENSIA

Advantage = AVANTAJE

After = DESPUES

After = DESPUES DE

After = DOSPUES

After = DOSPUES DE

Afterward = DOSPUES

Afterwards = DESPUES

Again = ANKORA

Against = KONTRA

Age = EDAD

Agency = ADJENSIA

Air = AYRE

Airplane = AVION

Aisle = KORIDOR

Alcohol = ALKOL

All [f.] = TODA

All [f.pl.] = TODAS

All [m.] = TODO

All [m.pl.] = TODOS

Almighty = ABASTÁDO

Almost = KAJI

Alphabet = ALEFBET

Already = PISHIN

Already = YA

Also = TAMBYEN

Alumnus = ELEVO

Always = SIEMPRE

Ambassador = AMBASADOR

America = AMERIKA

Ancient = AEDADO

And = I

Angel = ANDJELO

Anger = SEHORA

Animal = ANIMAL

Anise = ANITO

Another = OTRO

Antiquity = ANTIKITA

Apple = MANSANA

Appreciated = PRESIADO

April = AVRIL

Arab = ARABO

Arabic = ARABO

Arak (liquor) = RAKI

Argument = PELEA

Arm = BRASO

Army = ARMADA

Aroma = PARFUM

Around = ALDERREDOR

Arrow = FLECHA

As = KOMO

As well = TAMBYEN

Asparagus = ASPARAGO

Aspect = ASPEKTO

Aspirin = ASPIRIN

Ass [donkey] = AZNO

At a time = EN MIZMO TIEMPO

Attorney = AVOKATO

Aunt = TANTE

Aunt = TIA

Author = AUTOR

Automobile = OTOMOBIL

Autumn = OTONYO

Awake = ESPIERTO

Axe = BALTA

B

Back [of body] = ESPALDA

Back of = ATRAS

Bag = BOLSA

Bag = SAKO

Bald = KALAVASUDO

Bald = KALVO

Balloon = BALA

Banana = BANANA

Baseness = BASHEZA

Bathhouse = XAMAM

Beach = PLAJ

Bean = CHAUCHA

Beating = XAFTONA

Beautiful = ERMOZO

Beautiful = FERMOZO

Beautiful = FORMOZO

Beautiful = HERMOZO

Beautiful = YUZEL

Beautiful = LINDO

Beauty = ERMOZURA

Beauty = FERMOZURA

Beauty = ḤEN

Beauty = ḤENOZURA

Beauty = HERMOZURA

Because = POR KE

Because of = ACHAKES DE

Because of = POR

Because of = POR MODO DE

Because of this = POR ESTO

Beer = BIRA

Before = ANTES

Before = ANTES DE

Begger = SEDAKERO

Beginning = PRINSIPIO

Behind = ATRAS

Behold! = NA!

Beloved = KERIDO

Below = DEBASHO

Belt = KUSHAK

Belt = SINTURA

Belts = KUSHAKES

Best = LO MIJOR

Better = MIJOR

Better = MIJORADO

Between = ENTRE

Bicycle = BISIKLETA

Big (f.) = GRANDA

Big (m.) = GRANDE

Big fuss [person] = HADRAS I BARANAS

Bird = PASHARÓ

Birthday = ANIVERSARIO

Bitter = AMARGO

Black = MORENO

Black = PRETO

Bless you! [interj.] = BIVAS, KRESKAS, ENGRANDESKAS, KOMO UN PESHIKO EN AGUAS FRESKAS!

Blessed = BENDICHU / BENDICHO

Blessing = BERAXA

Blessing = ZAHUT

Blind = SIEGO

Blonde = BLONDO

Blower of the Ram's Horn = TOKEA

Blue = BLU

Body = PUERPO

Bone = GUESO

Book = LIVRO

Bookbinder = KOREX

Books = LIVROS

Borrowed = EMPRESTADO

Boss = KAPO

Boss = SHEF

Bottle = BOKAL

Bottle = RIDOMA

Boulevard = AVENIDA

Box = KASHA

Box, Big = KASHON

Boy = MANSEVO

Boy = MUCHACHO

Boy = NINYO

Boyfriend = NOVIO

Brain = MEOYO

Brand = MARKA

Bread = PAN

Bread = SIMIT

Breast = PECHO

Bride = NOVIA

Bridge = PONTE

Broth = KALDO

Brother [little] = ERMANIKO

Brother = ERMANO

Brothers [little] = ERMANIKOS

Brothers = ERMANIM

Brothers = ERMANOS

Brown = MORENO

Bull = TORO

Burnt = KEMADO

Bus = OTOBUS

Business = ECHO

Business = NEGOSIO

Busy = OKUPADO

But = MA [in general]

But = SINO [with negative constructions]

Butcher = KARNESERO

Butcher = KASAP

C

Cabin = KAMARA

Cake = PASTEL

Call = YAMADA

Calm = KALMO

Camel = GAMELLO

Candle = VELA

Capability = KAPACHEDAD

Capable = KAPACHI

Caprice = INNAT

Car = ARABA

Car = KOCHE

Carbon = KARVON

Careful = ATENSION

Careful = KUDIADO

Case = KAVZO

Casserole = CACHAROLE

Cat = GATO

Cave = MEARA

Cell [in prison] = SELULA

Cemetery Visit = ZIARA

Chair = SIYA

Character = KARAKTER

Charity = SEDAKA

Cheap = BARATO

Cheek = KARA

Cheese = KEZO

Chest = PECHO

Chicken = POYO

Chocolate = CHICOLATA

Christmas = NOEL

Cigarette = SIGARO

Cinema = SINEMA

City = SIVDAD

Civil = SIVIL

Class = KLASA

Classic = KLASIKO

Clean = LIMPIO

Clear = KLARO

Client = KLIENTE

Cloudy = BRUMOZO

Cloudy = NUVLOZO

Clown = PAYLACHO

Coffee House = KAVANÉ

Cold = YELADO

Collar = YAKÁ

Colony = KOLONIYA

Color = KOLOR

Colors = KOLORES

Combination = KOMBINASION

Comedy = KOMEDIA

Commandment = ENKOMENDANSA

Communities = KOMUNITAS

Community = KOMUNITA

Completely = KOMPLETAMENTE

Compliment = SHAKARUKA

Conclusion = KONKLUZION

Condemnation = KONDANASION

Conscience = KONSENSYA

Consequence = KONSEKUENSA

Consolation = KONSOLASION

Constant = KONSTANTE

Content [happy] = KONTENTE

Context = KONTEKSTO

Corner = KANTON

Corner = PUNTA

Corridor = KORIDOR

Country = PAIS

Country = PAYIS

Courtesy = POLITEZA

Cow = VAKA

Coward = ESPANTOZO

Crash = SHOK

Creature = KRIANSA

Creature = KRIATURA

Crime = KRIMEN

Crisis = KRIZA

Cultivated = KULTIVADO

Culture = KULTURA

Curiosity = KURIOZITA

Curiously = KURIOZAMENTE

Cursed = MALDICHO

Cute = LUZIO

D

Damned = MALDICHO

Dance = BAYLE

Dancer = BAYLADOR

Danger = PERIKOLO

Dangerous = PERIKOLOZO

Dangerously = PERIKOLOZAMENTE

Dark = ESKURO

Dark = MORENO

Darkness = ESKURIDAD

Date = DATA

Daughter = FIJA

Daughter-in-law = ERMUERA

Dauthers = FIJAS

Dawn = AMANESER

Day = DIA

Day = DIYA

Day before yesterday = ANTIYER

Day, all = DIA ENTERO

Dead = MUERTO

Dead = MET

Dead = NIFTAR

Dear = KARINYO

Death = MUERTE

December = DESIEMBRE

Deep = PROFUNDO

Delicious = DELISIOZO

Deluge = MAABE

Democracy = DEMOKRASIA

Dentist = DIENTISTO

Derived = DERIVADO

Desert = DEZIERTO

Desire = DEZEO

Destiny = DESTINO

Destiny = MAZAL

Detail = DETALYO

Devil = DIAVLO

Difference = DIFERENSIA

Difficult = ZOR

Difficulty = DIFIKULTAD

Dignity = DINYIDAD

Dinner = SENA

Direction = DIREKSION

Directly = DIREKTAMENTE

Dirt = EMBAKATÍNA

Dirty = EMBATAKADO

Dirty = SUZIO

Dizziness = SHASHEO

Doctor = DOKTOR

Doctor = MEDIKO

Dog = PERRO

Doll = KUKLA

Doll = PUSO

Dollar = DOLAR

Domestic = DOMESTIKO

Donkey = AZNO

Door = PUERTA

Dormitory = DORMITORIO

Doubt = DUBIO

Down = BASHO / BAXO

Down = ABASHO / ABÁSHO

Downpour = MAABE

Dream = ESUENYO

Dress = KOMPLE

Dress = KOSTUM

Dress = VESTIDO

Dressed properly = ḤENLI

Drug = DROGA

Drum = TAMBUR

Drunk = BORRACHO

Drunkard = BORRACHO

Duration = DURASION

During = DURANTE

During = DURANTE DE

E

Each = KADA

Ear = OREJA

Ear = OÍDO

Early = TEMPRANO

Easy = FASIL

Easy = KOLAY

Edge = KORTE

Edible = DE KOMER

Effect = EFEKTO

Egg = GUEVO

Eighth = OCHEN

Eleven = ONZE

Emerald = ESMERALDA

Employee = EMPIEGADO

Empty = VAZIYO

End = FIN

End = KAVO

Enjoyment = GUSTO

Enough already = YA BASTA

Entire = ENTERO

Entrance = ENTRADA

Equal = IGUAL

Equipment = BAGAJE

Error = FALTA

Europe = EVROPA

Event = MAASÉ

Everything = TODO

Evidence = PREVA

Evidence = PROVA

Evil = MAL

Evil = MALO

Exam = EGZAMEN

Example = EGZEMPIO

Excellent = EKSELENTE

Exception = EKSEPSION

Exercise = EGZERSIS

Exit = SALIDA

Expensive = KARO

Explanation = EKSPLIKASION

Explosion = EKSPLOZION

Exquisite = DELISIOZO

Eye [little] = OJIKO

Eye = OJO

Eye = OJO

Eyebrow = SEJA

Eyes [little] = OJIKOS

Eyes = OJOS

F

Face = FAZ

Face = KARA

Fairy = FADA

False = MENTIROZO

Family = FAMIYA

Famous = FAMOZO

Far = LESHOS

Fashion = MODO

Fat = GODRO

Father = PADRE

Fatigued = FATIGADO

Fatness = GODRURA

Fault = KULPA

Favor = FAVOR

Favor = HATIR

Fear = ESPANTO

Fear = MORÁ

Fed up = ARTO

Feeling = SENTIMIENTO

Fever = KAYENTURA

Field = CAMPO

Fifth = SINKEN

Fifty = SINKUENTA

Fig = IGO

Fight = PELEA

Figs = IGOS

Film = FILMO

Filth = EMBAKATÍNA

Finally = A LA FIN

Finally = FINALMENTE

Fine = FINO

Finger = DEDO

Fingers = DEDOS

First = PRIMERO

Fish (Seafood) = PESHKADO

Fist = PUNYO

Five = SINKO

Fix = FIKS

Flag = BANDIERA

Flame = FLAMA

Flan = KREM KARAMEK

Flavor = PASTO

Flavor = SAVOR

Flavorful = SAVROZO

Flea = PULGA

Floor = APARTAMENTO

Floor = ETAJ

Flour = ARINA

Flower = FLOR

Fly = MOSHKA

Fog = BRUMA

Fog = DUMAN

Fog = NEVLINA

Following = ASIGUN

Food = KOMIDA

Foolish act = AZNEDAD

Foolish thing = AZNEDAD

Foot = PIE

Football = FUTBOL

For = PARA

For = POR

Forehead = FAZ

Foreign = AJENO

Foreigner [f.] = AJENA

Foreigner = AJENO

Forest [Tropical] = SHARA TROPIKAL

Forest = SHARA

Forever = POR SIEMPRE

Fork = PIRON

Fork = PIRON

Form = FORMA

Former = ANTIKO

Fortunate = MAZALOZO

Foundation = FONDASION

Four = KUATRO

Fox = RENAR

Free = LIBERO

Free = LIBRE

Freedom = LIBERTAD

Freedom = ALFORRÍA

Freezer = CONJELADOR

French = FRANSEZ

Fresh = FRESKO

Fresh = FRESKO

Friend [f.] = AMIGA

Friend = AMIGO

Friendship = AMISTAD

Fruit = FRUTA

Full = YENO

Full of = YENO DE

Full of Joy = YENO DE DJOYA

Function = FONKSION

Funeral = ENTERRAMIENTO

Furniture = MOBLE

G

Garden = GUERTA

Gasoline = BENZIN

Gate = PUERTA

Gehenna = GINNAM

Gender = DJENERO

Generation = JENERASION

Generous = JENEROZO

Gentleman = SINYOR

Girl = NINYA

Girlfriend = NOVIA

Girlfriends = NOVIAS

Glass = VIDRO

Glasses = ANTOJOS

God = DIO

Gold = ORO

Good = BUENO

Goodbye! = ADYO!

Good News = HABERES BUENOS

Government = GOVERNO

Grace = GRASIA

Grace = ḤEN

Grace = ḤENOZURA

Grammar = GRAMER

Grandfather = GRANPAPA

Grandfather = NONO

Grandfather = PAPU

Grandmother = GRANMAMA

Grandmother = NONA

Grandmother = VAVA

Grandson = INYETO

Grass = YERVA

Gratefulness = AGRADESIMIENTO

Grave = ARÓN

Greece = GRESIA

Green = VEDRE

Grief = PENA

Grouchy person = AKSI BASHI

Ground = PATIN

Ground = SUELO

Guest = MUSAFIR

Guest = OSPITALIERO

Guide = GIADOR

Guilt = KULPA

Guitar = GITARA

Gum = CHIKLET

H

Habitual = ABITUAL

Hair = KAVEYO

Hair = PELO

Half = MEDIO

Half = MEATAD

Hamburger = HAMBURGER

Hand = LA MANO [f.]

Hand = MANO [f.]

Handkerchief = RIDA

Hands = LAS MANOS [f.]

Happiness = FELISIDA

Happy = ALEGRE

Happy = FELICHE

Happy = OROZO

Happy = MAZALOZO

Hard = DURO

Hat = CHAPEO

Hats = CHAPEOS

Have fun! = ENGLENEATE!

Hay = PAJA

He = EL

Head = KAVESA

Health = SALUD

Healthiness = SANEDAD

Heap = MONTON

Heart = KORASÓN

Hearts = KORASONES

Heat = KALOR

Heat = KALOR

Heaven = SYELO

Heavy = PEZGADO

Heavinesss = PEZGADURA

Hebrew = EBREO

Hell = GINNAM

Hell = INFERNO

Hen = GAYINA

Herb = YERVA

Here = AKI

Hero = EROE

High = ALTO

High = ALTO

History = ESTORIA

Hither = AKI

Holocaust = OLOKOSTO

Holy = SANTO

Holy = SAGRADO

Homemade = ECHIZO

Honey = MIEL

Honor = ONOR

Honor = KAVO

Honor = KAVOD

Hope = ESPERANSA

Hopefully = ISHALLA

Horrible = ORIVLE

Horse = KAVAYO

Hospital = OSPITAL

Hospitality = OSPITALIDAD

Hot = KAYENTE

Hot = KAÉNTE

Hour = ORA

House = KAZA

Houses = KAZAS

How! = KOMO

How much? = KAMMA

How much? = KUANTO

How many? = KAMMA

How many? = KUANTO

Humble = ANAV

Hunger = AMBRE

Hungry = AMBIERTO

Hurry = PRISA

Husband = MARIDO

Hymn = KANTIKA

I

I = YO

Ice = BUZ

Ice = YELO

Ice cream = AYISCRIN

Ice cream = YELADA

Idea = IDEA

Ignoramus = AMARES

Image = IMAJE

Immediately = IMEDIATAMENTE

Immense = IMENSO

Impacient = IMPASIENTE

Impediment = IMPEDIMIENTO

Important = EMPORTANTE

Impossible = EMPOSIVLE

In = EN

In addition = INDEMAS

In addition = POR DEMAZIYA

In front of = DELANTRE

In front of = DELANTRE DE

In front of = ENFRENTE

In front of = ENFRENTE DE

In general = JENERALMENTE

In the (m.) = ENEL

Incident = INSIDENTE

Included = INKLUZO

Inconvenient = INKONVENIVLE

Infancy = CHIKEZ

Inferior (f.) = INFERIORA

Inferior (m.) = INFERIOR

Infirm (f) = DOLIENTA

Infirm (m) = DOLIENTE

Influence = INFLUENSA

Influenza = ABASHADA

Information = INFORMASION

Informative = AVIZOS

Informative = NOVEDADES

Inheritance = ERENSIA

Inn = MOTEL

Innocent = INOSENTE

Inside of = ADIENTRO DE

Intelligent = INTELIJENTE

Intention = ENTISION

Interest = ENTERESO

Intestine = INTESTINO

Intimacy = INTIMIDAD

Introduction = INTRODUKSION

Investigation = INVESTIGASION

Invitation = INVITASION

Iron = FIERRO

Island = IZLA

Israel = ISRAEL

Israel = YISRAEL

Istanbul = ESTANBOL

It could be worse! [interj.] = KAPARA!

J

Jacket = DJAKETA

January = JENERO

Jealousy = EMBIDIA

Jem = DJOYA

Jewel = DJOYA

Jewish = DJUDEO

Jewish = DJUDIO

Jewish = YAHUDI

Jewish quarters = MAALÉ YAHUDI

Job = ECHO

Joke = ANEKDOTA

Joke = SHAKA

Judeo-Spanish Language = DJIDYO

Judeo-Spanish Language = DJUDEO-ESPANYOL

Judeo-Spanish Language = DJUDESMO

Judeo-Spanish Language = DJUDEZMO

Judeo-Spanish Language = DJUDYO

Judeo-Spanish Language = ESPANYOL

Judeo-Spanish Language = ESPANYOL SEFARDITA

Judeo-Spanish Language = LADINO

Judeo-Spanish Language = SEFARDÍ

Judeo-Spanish Language = DJUDEO-FRANYOL [dialect mixed with Italian and French]

Judge = DJUZGO

Juice = SUMO

K

Key = YAVE

Keys = YAVES

Killer = MATADOR

Killers = MATADORES

King = REY

Kingdom = REYNO

Kings = REYES

Kitchen = KOZINA

Kitchen = MUTPAK

Kitchens = KOZINAS

Kitchens = MUTPAKES

Knee = DIZ

Knees = DIZES

Knife = KUCHILYO

Knife = KUCHIYO

Knives = KUCHILYOS

Knives = KUCHIYOS

L

Labor = LAVORO

Laborer = LABORIOZO

Lady = MADAM

Lake = LAGO

Lake = RIO

Lamb = KODRERO

Land = TIERRA

Language = LINGUA

Languages = LINGUAS

Large (f.) = GRANDA

Large (m.) = GRANDE

Last = ULTIMO

Last night = ANOCHE

Late = TADRE

Law (religious) = DIN

Lawyer = AVOKATO

Laziness = HARAGANUD

Laziness = PAREZA

Lazy = HARAGAN

Lazy = INDECHIZO

Lazy = PARESOZO

Learning = APRENDIZAJE

Least = LO MINOR

Leek = PRASA

Left = SIEDRA

Lemon = LIMÓN

Lemons = LIMONES

Less = MANKO

Less = MANKO

Less = MENOS

Lesser = MINOR

Letter = LETRA

Letters = LETRAS

Level = NIVEL

Liar = MENTIROSO

License = LISENSIA

Lie = MENTIRA

Life = VIDA

Light = LUZ

Like = KOMO

Like that = ANSI

Like that = ANSINA

Like this = ANSI

Like this = ANSINA

Limit = LIMITO

Lip = MUSHO

Liver = FIGADO

Liver = HIGADO

Liver = LIGADO

Loneliness = SOLEDAD

Long = LARGO

Look = MIRADA

Love = AMOR

Lover = AMANTE

Low = BASHO / BAXO

Luck = SUERTE

Lungs = PULMONES

Luxurious = LUKSYOZO

Luxury = LUKSO

M

Mail = POSTA

Majorca = MAYORKA

Man = OMBRE

Manner = MANERA

Many = MUNCHO

Many = TANTO

Mark = MARKA

Matter = KOZA

Meaning = SINYIFIKASION

Measure = PREKOSION

Meat = KARNE

Medic = MEDIKO

Medication = KURA

Medicine = KURA

Medicine = MEDIKERIA

Medicine = MILIZINA

Memorable = MEMORAVLE

Memorable = MEMORAVLE

Memory = AKODRANSA

Memory = MEMORIA

Memory = TINO

Message = MESAJE

Midday = MEDIODIA

Midday = MIDI

Middle = MITAD

Middle-man = MATRAPÁS

Middle-men = MATRAPAZES

Midnight = MEDIANOCHE

Milk = LECHE

Million = MILYON

Miracle = MILAGRO

Miracle = MIRAKOLO

Mirror = ESPEJO

Mistake = FALTA

Mode = MODO

Molar = MUELA

Mom = MAMA

Moment = MOMENTO

Money = MONEDA

Money = PARA

Money = PARAS

Money-changer = SARAF

Month = MES

Months = MEZES

More = MAZ

Morning = AMANYANA

Morning = DEMANYANA

Morning, Early = MADRUGADA

Motel = MOTEL

Mother = MADRE

Motorcycle = MOTOSIKLETA

Mountain = MONTANYA

Moustache = MUSTACHO

Mouth = BOKA

Mouths = BOKAS

Movie = FILMO

Much = MUNCHO

Much = TANTO

Mushroom = SHAMPINYON

Music = MUZIKA

Mutually = UNO A OTRO

N

Nail = UNYA

Name = NOMBRE

Names = NOMBRES

Nape = PISKUESO

Nation = NASYON

National = NASIONAL

Nature = NATURA

Near = SERKA

Near = SERKANO

Necessary = NESESARIO

Neck = GARGANTA

Need = NESESIDAD

Negative = NEGATIVO

Neighbor = VEZINO

Neighbor = VIZINO

Neighborhood = MAALÉ

Neither = NI…NI

Neither…nor = NI

Nervous = INYERVOZO

Nest = NIDO

Never = NUNKA

New = MUEVO

New = NUEVO [dialectal]

News = XABER

News = HABER

News = HABERES

News = XABERES

Newspaper = JURNAL [dzhur-nal]

Next [f.] = LA DE DESPUES

Next [f.pl.] = LAS DE DESPUES

Next [m.] = EL DE DESPUES

Next [m.pl.] = LOS DE DESPUES

Night = NOCHE

Nightingale = BIBILIKO

Nightingales = BIBILIKOS

No one = DINGUNO

Nobody = DINGUNO

Nobody = NINGUNO

Noise = BRUIDO

Nonsense! [interj.] = BAVAJADAS!

Normal = ABITUAL

Nose = NARIZ

Nostalgia = NOSTALJIA

Not = NO

Not = NON

Not any = DINGUNO

Notably = NOTAVLAMENTE

Notebook = TEFTER

Nothing = NADA

Nothingness = VAZIDURA

Notice = AVIZO

Now = AGORA

O

Obedient = OBEISENTE

Obedient = OVEDESYENTE

Obedient = ANAV

Obesity = GODRURA

Object = OBJEKTO

Obligation = OVLIGASION

Obscure = ESKURO

Obscurity = ESKURIDAD

Obstacle = OBSTAKOLO

Occasion = OKAZION

Odor = GOLOR

Of = DE

Of course = NATURALMENTE

Of the World = MUNDIAL

Of which? = DONDE?

Of whom? = DONDE?

Office = BURO

Office = OFISIO

Official = OFISIAL

Oil = AZETE

Old = AEDADO

Old = ANTIKO

Old [m] = VIEJO

Old [f] = VIEJA

Olive = ASETUNA

Olive Tree = ASETUNAL

Olives = ASETUNAS

One's Own = APROPIADO

Onion = SEVOYA

Only [adj.] = REGALADO

Only = SOLAMENTE

Only = SOLO

Opening = AVYERTURA

Opinion = OPINION

Opportunity = OPORTUNIDAD

Orange = PORTOKAL

Orchard = BOSTAN

Orchard = GUERTO

Order = ORDEN

Ordinary = BAYAGI

Ordinary = ORDINARIO

Other = OTRO

Others = OTROS

Our = MUESTRO

Our = NUESTRO [dialectal]

Out of = AFUERA DE (AHUERA DE)

Out of = FUERA DE (HUERA DE)

Outside = AFUERA (AHUERA)

Outside = FUERA (HUERA)

Oven = FORNO

Oven = HORNO

Over = ENDRIVA

Over = ENRIVA

Over = SOVRE

Owl = KUKUVAYA

Owner = PATRON

Owner = PROPRIETARIO

Oy! = GUAY DE MI!

Oyster = ESTRIDIA

P

Page = OJA

Pain = DOLOR

Pain = DOLOR

Pains = DOLORES

Painter = PINTADOR

Painting = TABLO

Papa = PAPA

Paper = PAPEL

Paradise = GANEDEN

Parsley = MAYDANOZ

Part = PARTE

Party = FIESTA

Passenger = PASAJERO

Passion = ARDOR

Passport = PASAPORTO

Past = PASADO

Path = KAMINO

Patience = PASENSIA / PASENSYA

Peace = PAS

Peach = SHEFTELI

Peasant = AMARES

Pen = STILO

Pencil = KALEM

People = DJENTE

People = DJENTE

People = PERSONAS

Perfect = PERFEKTO

Perfection = PERFEKSION

Person = PERSONA

Person = PERSONA

Pharmacy = FARMASIYA

Philosophy = FILOZOFIA

Photography = FOTOGRAFIA

Phrase = FRAZA

Piece = PEDASO

Pineapple = ANANAS

Place = LUGAR

Places = LUGARES

Plate = PLATO

Plate = CHINI

Pleasure = PLAZER

Pleasure = GANA

Plenty = MABUL

Pocket = ALDIKERA

Poetry = POEZIA

Police = POLISIYA

Police = POLIS

Pool = PISINA

Poor = POVERETO

Poor = PROVE

Popular = POPULAR

Position = KONTUAR

Positive = POZITIVO

Possession = POSESION

Possibility = POSIBLIDAD

Possible = POSIVLE

Potato = PATATA

Powder = POLVORA

Power = PODER

Prayer = ORASION

Prayer = TEFILÁ

Precise = PRECHIZO

Precisely = PRECHIZAMENTE

Preferred = ENVELUNTADO

Pregnant [f. only] = PRENYADA

Preparation = PREPARATIVOS

Preposition = PREPOZISION

Prescription = RECHETA

Prescription = RESEFTA

Present = PREZENTE

Pretty = ERMOZO

Pretty = FERMOZO

Pretty = FORMOZO

Pretty = HERMOZO

Pretty = LINDO

Pretty = LUZIO

Price = PRESIO

Pride = ORGOLYO

Princess = PRENSESA

Problem = PROBLEM

Problems = PENSERIOS

Professional = PROFESIONAL

Profile = PERFIL

Profile = PROFIL

Program = PROGRAMA

Prohibited = ASUR

Project = PRODJEKTO

Prompt = ḤENLI

Proof = PREVA

Proof = PROVA

Proverb = REFRÁN

Proverb = PROVERBIO

Proverbs = REFRANES

Proverbs = PROVERBIOS

Province = PROVENSIA

Public = PUBLIKO

Purim = PURIM

Purim present = PURIMLIK

Q

Question = DEMANDA

Question = KESTION

Question = PREGUNTA

Quick = RAPIDO

Quicker = MAZ RAPIDO

Quickly = RAPIDAMENTE

Quiet [interj.] = KAYADES!

R

Rabbi = HAHAM

Rabbi = ḤAḤAM

Race = RASA

Racism = RASIZMO

Railroad = SHEMIN-DE-FER

Rain = LUVIA

Rare = RALO

Rat = RATON

Reader = LEKTOR

Reading = MELDADURA

Really = REALMENTE

Reason = MEOYO

Reason = RAZON

Rebellion = REBELION

Receipt = RECHETA

Receipt = RESEFTA

Red = KOLORADO

Red = KOLERADO

Red-haired = RUVIO

Region = REJION

Religion = RELIJION

Remedy = DEMEDIO

Remedy = REMEDIO

Repeated = REPETIDO

Report = REPORTAJE

Republic = REPUBLIKA

Respect = RESPEKTO

Responsibility = RESPONSABILITAD

Restaurant = RESTORANTE

Restless = INKIETO

Revenge = VENGANSA

Reverse = A LA ROVES

Revolution = REVOLUSION

Rice = ARROZ

Rice pudding = SUTLACH

Rich = RIKO

Riddle = ROMPEKAVESA

Risk = RIZIKO

River = RIO

Rocket = ROKETA

Roof = TECHO

Room = KAMARETA

Rooster = GAYO

Root = RAIS

Rule = REGLA

Rules = DINIM

S

Sabbath = SHABAT

Sacrifice = SAKRIFISIO

Sad = TRISTE

Saffron = ALSAFRAN

Salad = SALATA

Sale = VENDIDA

Same = MISMO

Same = MIZMO

Same, the [f.pl.] = UNAS

Same, the [m.pl.] = UNOS

Satisfied = SATISFECHO

Savage = SALVAJE

Scene = SHENA

School = ESKOLA

Science = SENSIA

Scream = GRITO

Sea = MAR

Search = BUSHKIDA

Seat = ASENTADOR

Second [adj.] = SEGUNDO

Secret = SEKRETO

Secretly = A LAS ESKONDIDAS

Security = SEGURIDAD

Sefardi Jews = SEFARDIM

Selfish = EGOISTO

Serpent = KULEVRA

Servant = MESHARED

Servants = MESHAREDIM

Sesame = SESAMO

Sex = SEKSO

Shade = SOLOMBRA

Shame = PEKADO

Shawl = SHAL

She = EYA

Ship = NAVE

Ship = VAPOR

Shirt = KAMIZA

Shit = MEDRA

Shoe = KALSADO

Shoe = SAPATO

Shoes = CHAPINES

Shop = BODRUM

Shop = MAGAZEN

Short = KURTO

Shotgun = FUZIL

Shotgun = TUFENK

Shoulder = OMBRO

Shower = DUSH

Shy = TIMIDO

Sick (f) = DOLIENTA

Sick (m) = DOLIENTE

Sick = HAZINO

Sickly = DOLENTIO

Sickness = HAZINURA

Side = LADO

Silence = SILENSIO

Silver = PLATA

Since = DESDE

Since = DESDE DE

Sincere = SINSERO

Single = SOLTERO

Sister [little] = ERMANIKA

Sister = ERMANA

Sisters [little] = ERMANIKAS

Sisters = ERMANAS

Site = SITIO

Situation = SITUASION

Six = SEIS [sesh]

Skinny = FLAKITO

Skinny = FLAKO

Skirt = FUSTA

Sky = SYELO

Slaughter = SHEHITAH

Slaughter = SHEḤITAH

Sleepy = KANSADO

Sleeve = MANGA

Slowly = AVAGAR

Slowly = AVARIGO

Slowly = LENTAMENTE

Small = CHIKO

Smell = GOLOR

Snake = KULEVRA

Snow = INYEVE

So = TAN

So that = PARA KE

Soap = SHAVON

Social = SOSYAL

Soda = GAZOZA

Soldier = SOLDADO

Some (f.pl.) = UNAS

Some (m.pl.) = UNOS

Something = ALGO

Son [little] = IJIKO

Son = FIJO

Son = HIJO

Song = KANTIKA

Sons [little] = IJIKOS

Sons = FIJOS

Sons = HIJOS

Soon = PRESTO

Soul = ALMA

Sound = BOZ

Sound = SONETE

Soup = SUPA

Space = ESPASIO

Spain = ESPANYA

Spanish = ESPANYOL

Special = ESPESIAL

Speech = FAVLA

Spicy = PIKANTE

Spoken = FAVLADO

Spool of thread = MACHARÁ

Spoon = KUCHARA

Stairs = ESKALERAS

Star = ESTREYA

Star = MAZAL

Stars [coll.] = ESTRELLERIA / ESTREYERIA

State = ESTADO

Station (of Gas) = ESTASION DE BENZIN

Station = ESTASION

Steak = BIFTEK

Stealthily = A LAS EKONDIDAS

Still = DAÍNDA

Stomach = ESTOMAGO

Store = BODRUM

Store = BOTIKA

Storm = FURTUNA

Storm = TEMPESTA

Story = MAASÉ

Strange = ESTRANYO

Straw = PAJA

Street = KAYE

Street = MAALÉ

Strong = FUERTE

Study Hall = MIDRASH

Stupid = BOVO

Stupidity = BOVEDAD

Stutterer = PELTEK

Subject = SUJETO

Suddenly = EN SUPITO

Suddenly = ENSUPITO

Sugar = ASUKAR

Suitcase = VALIDJA

Summer = ENVERANO

Sun = SOL

Sunday = ALHAD / ALHÁT

Sunny = SOLEADO

Supermarket = SUPERMARKET

Supper = SENA

Surname = ALKUNYA

Surrounded = ENTORNADO

Sweet = DULSE

Sword = ESPADA

Syllabary = SILIBARYO

Syllable = SILABA

Synagogue = KAHAL

Synagogue = KAḤAL

Synagogue = KAL

Synagogue = KEHILÁ

Synagogue = KEILÁ

Synagogues = KAHALIM

Synagogues = KAḤALIM

Synagogues = KALIM

Synagogues = KEHILAS

Synagogues = KEHILOT

Synagogues = KEILAS

Synagogues = KEILOT

System = SISTEMA

T

Table = MEZA

Tale = KUENTO

Tall = ALTO

Tank = TANK

Tea = CHAY

Teacher = MAESTRO

Teacher [at university] = PROFESOR

Temporary = TEMPORALMENTE

Ten = DIEZ

Terrible = TERRIVLE

Test = EGZAMEN

Thankfulness = AGRADESIMIENTO

Thanks = SHUKUR

Thank you! = GRASIAS! / GRASYAS!

That [conj.] = KE

That [conj.] = KE

That [f.] = ESTA

That [m.] = ESTE

That [over there] = AKEYO

That which [conj.] = LO KE

The (f.pl.) = LAS

The (f.sing.) = LA

The (m.pl.) = LOS

The (m.sing.) = EL

Theater = SINEMA

Theater = TEATRO

Theme = SUJETO

Then = ALORA

Then = DUNKE

Then = PORTANTO

There = AYA

There = AYI

Therefore = DUNKE

They (f.) = EYAS

They (m.) = EYOS

Thief = LADRON

Thieves = LADRONIM

Thing = KOZA

Thirst = SER

This [f.] = ESTA

This [m.] = ESTE

This morning = OY DEMANYANA

Thought = PENSADA

Thousand = MIL

Three = TRES

Thursday = DJUGEVES

Tickles = KOSHKIYAS

Tie = KRAVATA

Time = TIEMPO

Time = VEZ

Times = VECES

Tired = KANSADO

Tiredness = KANSERYA

Title = TITOLO

To = A

To the Contrary = AL KONTRARIO

To where? = ANDE

Today = OY

Together = DJUNTOS

Together = ENDJUNTOS

Toilet = TUALETA

Tomato = TOMAT

Tomorrow = AMANYANA

Tomorrow = DEMANYANA

Tongue = LINGUA

Tongues = LINGUAS

Too [adj.] = DEMAZIADO

Tooth = DIENTE

Torrent = MAABE

Tough = REZIO

Towards = VERSO

Town = KAZAL

Toy = DJUGETE

Traffic = TRAFIKO

Tragedy = TRAJEDIA

Train = TRENO

Tranquil = KALMO

Translator = TRADUKTOR

Travel = VIAJE

Treasure = TREZORO

Tree = ARVOLE

Tree = AACH

Trial = PREVA

Trial = PROVA

Trunk = BAUL

Trust = KONFIENSA

Truth = VEDRA

Truth = VERDAD

Turkey = TURKIA

Twelve = DODJE

Twenty = VENTE

Two = DOS

Two hundred = DOZIENTOS

Type = TIPO

U

Ugly = FEO

Umbrella = CHADIR

Uncle = TIO / TÍO

Underneath = DEBASHO

Unit = UNIDAD

United = UNIDO

Universal = UNIVERSAL

University = UNIVERSITA

Until = ASTA

Up = ARRIVA / ARRÍVA

Upon = ENDRIVA

Upon = ENRIVA

Upon = SOVRE

V

Vacation = VAKANSAS

Vase = KUPA

Vegetable = ZARZAVAT

Velocity = PRESTOR

Vengeance = VENGANSA

Very = MUY

Victim = VIKTIMA

Victory = VIKTORIA

Village = KAZAL

Village = PUEVLO

Villager = KAZALINO

Vineyard = VINYA

Visit = VIJITA

Vitamin = VITAMINA

Voice = BOZ

Voices = BOZES

Voluntary = VELUNTARIO

Volunteer = VELUNTARIO

Vowel = VOKAL

W

Waist = BEL

Waiter = GARSON

Waiter = MOSO

Wall = PARED

War = GERRA

Wasp = BIZBA

Watch = ORA DE BRAZO

Water = AGUA

Watermelon = KARPUZ / KARPUS

Way = KAMINO

We (1st pl. f.) = MOZÁS

We (1st pl. f.) = MOZOTRAS

We (1st pl. f.) = NOZOTRAS

We (1st pl. m.) = MOZÓS

We (1st pl. m.) = MOZOTROS

We (1st pl. m.) = NOZOTROS

Weak = FLAKO

Weak = SIN FUERSA

Weapon = ARMA

Week = SEMANA

Weekend = FIN DE SEMANA

Weekly = POR SEMANA

Weight = PEZGO

Well = BYEN

West = MAARÁV

What = KE

What's new? = KE HABER?

What's up? = KE HABER?

When [adv.] = KUANDO

When [conj.] KUANDO

Where? = ANDE?

Where [from] = DE ANDE?

Where [to] = ANDE?

Which (f.) = KUALA

Which (m.) = KUALO

Whichever = KUALKIER / -A

While = MIENTRES

While = TIEMPO

Whim =INNAT

White = BLANKO

Whither? = ANDE?

Who? = KEN

Whose = KE TIENE

Whose = DONDE

Why = PORKE

Wife = ESPOZA

Will = VELUNTAD

Will = VOLUNTAD

Wind = AYRE

Window = VENTANA

Wine = VINO

Wine, Red = VINO KOLORADO

Wine, White = VINO BLANKO

Wise = SEZUDO

Wishing = VELUNTOZO

With = KON

With me = KON MI

With you = KON TI

Without = SIN

Woe = GUAY

Wolf = LOVO

Woman = MUJER [muzh-er]

Woman, Sultan's favorite = HASAKI

Women = MUJERES [muzh-er-es]

Wood = SHARA

Word = BIERVO

Word = PALAVRA

Words = PALAVRAS

Work [of art or literature] = OVRA

Work = ECHO

Work = LAVORO

Worker = LABORIOZO

World = MUNDO

Worm = GUZANO

Worried = PREOKUPADO

Worry = PREOKUPASION

Worse = MAS MAL

Y

Year = ANYADA

Year = ANYO

Years = LAS ANYADAS

Yell = GRITO

Yellow = AMARIYO

Yes = SI

Yesterday = AYER

You (2nd pl. f.) = VOZÁS

You (2nd pl. f.) = VOZOTRAS

You (2nd pl. m.) = VOZÓS

You (2nd pl. m.) = VOZOTROS

You (2nd sing.) = TU

Young = DJOVEN

Your = TU

Youth = CHIKÉS [f.]

Yugoslavia = YUGOSLAVIA

Z

Zeal = SELO

Zodiac = ZODIAKO

Useful Judeo-Spanish verbs:

Format: English Verb = Judeo-Spanish Verb

English – Judeo-Spanish

Abandon = ABANDONAR

Abhor = ABORRESER

Accept = AKSEPTAR

Accepted, Have = AVER AKSEPTADO

Accomodate = AKOMODAR

Accompany = AKOMPANYAR

Accustom = AKOSTUMBRAR

Achieve = KOMPLIR

Achieve = KUMPLIR

Achieve = OBTENER

Achieve = PARVENIR

Administer = ADMINISTRAR

Admire = ADMIRAR

Advance = AVANSAR

Advance = PROGRESAR

Advise = KONSEJAR

Agree = AKORDAR

Agree = AKORDARSE

Alarm = ALARMAR

Allow = DESHAR

Allow = PERMETER

Animate = ENKORAJAR

Appear = APARESER

Arrange = ATAKANEAR

Arrest = ARRESTAR

Arrive = ARRIVAR

Arrive = AYEGAR

Ask = DEMANDAR

Ask = PRUNTAR

Ask for = DEMANDAR

Ask Question = DEMANDAR

Ask Question = PRUNTAR

Asked, Have = AVER PRUNTADO

Assist = ASISTIR

Attach = ADJUNTAR

Attack = ATAKAR

Attend = ASISTIR

Augur = OGURAR

Await = ESPERAR

Awaited, Have = AVER ESPERADO

Awaken = DESPERTAR

Awakened, Have = AVER DESPERTADO

Be = ESTAR

Be = SER

Be Able to = PUEDER

Be Born = NASER

Be Careful = AZER ATANSION

Be Careful = ECHAR TINE

Be Dazed = SHASHEARSE

Be Successful = REUSHIR

Be Sufficient = ABASTAR

Be Worth = VALER

Bear = SOMPORTAR

Beat = AXARVAR

Beatify = AHENAR

Beatify = AHENOZEAR

Beautify = AFERMOZIGUAR

Beautify = AFORMOZIGUAR

Beautify = FERMOZIGUAR

Been, Have = AVER ESTADO

Been, Have = AVER SIDO

Beg = ARROGAR

Beg = MENDIKAR

Beg = ROGAR

Begin = EMPESAR

Begin = INISIAR

Begun, Have = AVER EMPESADO

Believe = KREYER

Believe in = ENFEUZIAR

Believed, Have = AVER KREYIDO

Benefit = PROFITAR

Bless = BENDIZIR

Blessed, Have = AVER BENDICHO / BENDICHU

Blow away = ASOPLAR

Blow on = ASOPLAR

Boil = BUYIR

Bore = ENFASYAR

Bother = FISHUGAR

Bother = MOLESTAR

Bought, Have = AVER MERKADO

Brandish = MENEAR

Break = ROMPER

Break up = ALESHAR

Bring = TRAER

Bring = YEVAR

Bring = KITAR

Broken, Have = AVER ROTO

Brought, Have = AVER TRAYIDO

Brought, Have = AVER YEVADO

Build = FRAGUAR

Build = KONSTRUIR

Built, Have = AVER FRAGUADO

Burn = KEMAR

Bury = ENTERRAR

Buy = MERKAR

Call = YAMAR

Care for = KUDIAR

Caress = KARESAR

Carried, Have = AVER YEVADO

Carry = YEVAR

Catch = AFERRAR

Caught, Have = AVER AFERRADO

Cause = KAVZAR

Change = TROKAR

Changed, Have = AVER TROKADO

Chew = MASHKAR

Choose = ESKOJER

Chose, Have = AVER ESKOJIDO

Close = SERRAR

Closed, Have = AVER SERRADO

Coincide = KOENSIDAR

Collect = ARREKOJER

Collect = REKOJER

Collected, Have = ARREKOJIDO

Collected, Have = REKOJIDO

Comb one's Hair = PEYNARSE

Come = VENIR

Come close = ASERKAR

Come close = ASERKARSE

Come, Have = AVER VENIDO

Command = ORDENAR

Communicate = KOMUNIKAR

Complain = KESHARSE

Compliment = AZER SHAKARUKA

Conduct = KONDUZIR

Confirm = KONFIRMAR

Confront = AFRENTAR

Confront = AFRONTAR

Confuse = KONFONDER

Conquer = KONKUISTAR

Consent = KONSENTIR

Console = KONSOLAR

Contain = KONTENER

Contain = KONTENERSE

Contained, Have = AVER KONTENIDO

Contemplate = KONTEMPLAR

Continue = KONTINUAR

Continue onward = ADELANTAR

Convince = KONVENSER

Cook = KOZER

Cost = KOSTAR

Cover = KUVIJAR

Cover = KUVRIR

Cover with boards = ENTAVLAR

Crash = CHAPTEAR

Create = KREAR

Created, Have = AVER KREADO

Cross = PASAR ENFRENTE

Cry = LYORAR

Cry = YORAR

Curse = MALDEZIR

Curse = MALDIZIR

Cut = KORTAR

Cut, Have = AVER KORTADO

Dance = BAYLAR

Dare = OZAR

Darken = ESKURESERSE

Dawn = AMANESER

Decide = DECHIDIR

Decide = DESIDAR

Decided, Have = AVER DESIDADO

Decorate = AḤENOZEAR

Dedicate = DEDIKARSE

Defend = DEFENDER

Defend oneself = DEFENDERSE

Demonstrate = DEMOSTRAR

Demonstrated, Have = AVER DEMOSTRADO

Deny = ENYEGAR

Depend = DEPENDER

Deserve = MERESER

Desire = DEZEYAR

Destroy = DERROKAR

Destroy = DESTRUIR

Detain = DETENER

Develop = DEZVELOPAR

Developed, Have = AVER DEZVELOPADO

Devour = DEVORAR

Die = MURIR

Died, Have = AVER MUERTO

Discover = DESKUVIJAR

Discover = DESKUVRIR

Discuss = DISKUTIR

Dispatch = ESPEDIR

Dispose of = DISPOZAR

Distinguish = DISTINGUIR

Disturb = FISHUGAR

Disturb = MOLESTAR

Do [make reality] = REALIZAR

Do = AZER

Do = FAZER

Do again = TORNAR I

Do again = VOLVER

Done again, Have = AVER VUELTO

Done, Have = AVER ECHO

Done, Have = FECHO

Done, Have just = VENIR DI

Double = DUBLAR

Draw = DESINAR

Dream = SONYAR

Dress = VESTIR

Dress oneself = VESTIRSE

Drink = BEVER

Drunk, Have = AVER BEVIDO

Dry = SEKAR

Eat = KOMER

Eat Dinner = SENAR

Eat Lunch = KOMER POR MIDI

Eaten, Have = AVER KOMIDO

Elect = ELIJIR

Elected, Have = AVER ELIJIDO

Embitter = AMARGAR

Embittered, Have = AVER AMARGADO

Embrace = ABRASAR

Embraced, Have = AVER ABRASADO

Encounter = TOPAR

Encourage = ENKORAJAR

End = TERMINAR

Endow = ENGRACIAR

Endure = TURAR

Enjoy = GOZAR

Enter = ENTRAR

Erase = BARRAR

Erase = EFASAR

Establish = ESTABLESER

Examine = EGZAMINAR

Exchange = TROKAR

Exchanged, Have = AVER TROKADO

Excuse = ESKUZAR

Exist = EGZISTIR

Expand = ESPANDIR

Expel = ARONDJAR

Expelled, Have = AVER ARONDJADO

Experiment = EKSPERIMENTAR

Expire = MURIR

Explain = EKSPLIKAR

Explain in Ladino = ENLADINAR

Explain in Ladino = LADINAR

Explained, Have = AVER EKSPLIKADO

Explode = EKSPLOZAR

Explore = EKSPLORAR

Expose = EKSPOZAR

Express = EKSPRESAR

Extinguish = AMATAR

Fall = KAYER

Fallen, Have = AVER KAYIDO

Fatten up = ENGODRAR

Fear = TENER TEMOR

Feed = ALIMENTAR

Feel = SENTIRSE

Feel = SINTIR

Feel well = SENTIRSE BYEN

Felt, Have = AVER SENTIDOSE

Fill = INCHIR

Find = ENKONTRAR

Find = TOPAR

Find out = INFORMARSE

Find out = TOMAR HABER

Finish = AKAVAR

Fish = PESHKAR

Flee = FUYIR

Fold = DUBLAR

Follow = SIGUIR

Followed, Have = AVER SIGUIDO

Force in = ENKASHAR

Forget = ECHAR EN OLVIDO

Forget = OLVIDAR

Forget = OLVIDARSE

Forgive = DISKULPAR

Forgive = ESKUZAR

Forgotten, Have = AVER ECHADO EN OLVIDO

Forgotten, Have = AVER OLVIDADO

Found, Have = AVER ENKONTRADO

Fry = FRIYIR

Gather = ARREKOJER

Gather = REKOJER

Get = OBTENER

Get better = MIJORAR

Get dark = ESKURESERSE

Get dirty = EMBATAKAR

Get dirty = EMBATAKARSE

Get dirty = ENSUZIAR

Get dressed = VISTIRSE

Get in [the car] = SUBERSE

Get near = ASERKAR

Get near = ASERKARSE

Get up = ALEVANTAR

Gift giving = ARREGLAMIENTO

Give = DAR

Give a gift = ARREGALAR

Give a gift = AZER REGALO

Give Birth = METER AL MUNDO

Give birth = PARIR

Give up = RENDERSE

Given, Have = AVER DADO

Glorify = AFERMOZIGUAR

Glorify = AFORMOZIGUAR

Glorify = FERMOZIGUAR

Go = IR

Go = ANDAR

Go away = SALIR

Go crazy = ENLOKESER

Go down = ABASHAR

Go down = ABAXAR

Go forward = ADELANTAR

Go out = SALIR

Go shopping = IR DE KOMPRAR

Go to = IR A

Go to Bed = ECHARSE

Go to Bed = ESPANDIRSE

Gone away, Have = AVER SALIDO

Gone out, Have = AVER SALIDO

Gone, Have = AVER IDO

Grow = ENGRANDESER

Grow = KRESER

Grow up = ENGRANDESER

Guard = GUADRAR

Guide = ORIENTAR

Had, Have = AVER TENIDO

Hang = ENKOLGAR

Hang = PENDER

Happen = AKONTESER

Happen = SUKSEDAR

Hate = ABORRESER

Have = AVER

Have = TENER

Have fun = DIVERTIRSE

Have fun = EGLENEARSE

Have to = DEVER

Heal = SANARSE

Hear = OYIR

Heard, Have = AVER OYIDO

Heat = KAYENTAR

Heated, Have = AVER KAYENTADO

Help = AYUDAR

Helped, Have = AVER AYUDADO

Hide = ESKONDERSE

Hide = ESKONDIR

Hit = AHARVAR

Hold = KONTENER

Hold onto = KONTENER

Hope = ASPERAR

Hope = ESPERAR

Hope = ESPERAR

Hope = ESPERAR

Hoped, Have = AVER ESPERADO

Hug = ABRASAR

Hugged, Have = AVER ABRASADO

Hurry = APRESURARSE

Hurt = ERGUELER

Hurt = FERIR

Imagine = IMAJINAR

Impede = EMPEDIR

Impede = IMPEDIR

Impose = FORSAR

Improve = ABONIGUAR

Incline = ENKLINAR

Include = INKLUIR

Increase = AMOCHIGUAR

Increase = AUMENTAR

Increase = MUCHIGUAR

Inform = INFORMAR

Injure = FERIR

Insert = ENKASHAR

Insult = AFRENTAR

Insult = AFRONTAR

Intensify = INTENSIFIKAR

Interest = ENTERESARSE

Interrupt = ENTEROMPER

Introduce = INTRODUZIR

Invent = ENVENTAR

Invest = INVESTIR

Invite = ENVITAR

Invite = INVITAR

Invited, Have = AVER INVITADO

Irrigate = ARRUFIAR

Jump = SALTAR

Just did something [present] = AKAVAR DE

Keep = GUADRAR

Keep warm = ABRIGARSE

Kill = MATAR

Killed, Have = AVER MATADO

Kneel = ARRODIYAR

Kneel = ENGINOLYAR

Kneel = ENRODIYAR

Know = SAVER

Know Someone = KONESER

Know Someone = KONOSER

Known someone, Have = AVER KONESIDO

Known someone, Have = AVER KONOSIDO

Known, Have = AVER SAVIDO

Lack = FALTAR

Lack = MANKAR

Last = TURAR

Laugh = REIR

Launch = LANSAR

Learn = AMBEZAR

Learn = AMBEZARSE

Learned, Have = AVER AMBEZADO

Learned, Have = AVER AMBEZADOSE

Leave = DESHAR

Leave = PARTIR

Leave = SALIR

Left, Have = AVER PARTIDO

Left, Have = AVER SALIDO

Let = DESHAR

Lick = LAMBER

Light = ASENDER

Lighten = ASENDER

Lighten = ENSENDER

Like = AGRADAR

Like to = AGRADAR A

Like to = PLAZER A

Listen = ESCUCHAR

Listen = OYIR

Listened, Have = AVER ESCUCHADO

Live = BIVIR

Live = MORAR

Lived, Have = AVER BIVIDO

Lived, Have = AVER MORADO

Load = KARGAR

Look = VERSE

Look = MIRAR

Look for = BUSKHAR

Looked for, Have = AVER BUSKHADO

Loosen = AFLOSHAR

Lose = PEDRER

Lose = PEDRER

Lose = PIEDRER

Lost, Have = AVE PEDRIDO

Lower = ABASHAR

Lower = ABAXAR

Made Dirty, Have = AVER ENSUZYADO

Maintain = MANTENER

Make a vow = DJURAR

Make Better = ABONIGUAR

Make Dirty = ENSUZYAR

Make Mistake = YERRARSE

Make sure = ASEGURAR

Marry = KASAR

Marry = KAZAR

Marvel = MARAVIYARSE

Mean = SIGNIFIKAR

Mean = SINYIFIKAR

Meant, Have = AVER SIGNIFIKADO

Measure = MESURAR

Meditate = MEDITAR

Meet = ENKONTRARSE

Met, Have = AVER ENKONTRADOSE

Mix = MESKLAR

Moderate oneself = ARRESENTARSE

Moisten = MOJAR

Move = METER EN MOVIMIENTO

Move = MOVER

Move = MUDAR

Moved, Have = AVER MUDADO

Moved, Have = MOVIDO

Multiply = AMOCHIGUAR

Multiply = MUCHIGUAR

Must = DEVER

Narrate = KONTAR

Narrated, Have = AVER KONTADO

Need = NESESITAR

Need = TENER MENESTER

Needed, Have = AVE NESESITADO

Obligate = OVLIGAR

Observe = OBSERVAR

Obstruct = EMBARASAR

Obtain = OBTENER

Occur = AKONTESER

Offer = OFRESER

Offer = OFRIR

Offer = PROPOZAR

Offered, Have = AVER OFIERTO

Offered, Have = AVER PROPOZADO

Open = AVRIR

Opened, Have = AVER AVIERTO

Operate = OPERAR

Oppose = OPOZAR

Oppress = OPRIMIR

Orient = ORIENTAR

Overthrow = DERROKAR

Overwhelm = OPRIMIR

Paid, Have = AVER PAGADO

Paint = BOYADEAR

Painted, Have = AVER BOYADEADO

Participate = PARTISIPAR

Party = FIESTAR

Pass = PASAR

Passed, Have = AVER PASADO

Pay = PAGAR

Pay = PAGAR

Peel = MUNDAR

Permit = PERMETER

Persuade = KONVENSER

Place = METER

Place = POZAR

Place = SITUAR

Placed, Have = AVER METIDO

Play = DJUGAR

Play = JUGAR [zhu-gar]

Played, Have = AVER DJUGADO

Played, Have = AVER JUGADO

Plead = ARROGAR

Please = KONTENTAR

Please = PLAZER

Pleasure = PLAZER

Pledge = PROMETER

Portray = AZER PORTRETO

Possess = POSEDAR

Practice = PRATIKAR

Pray = ARROGAR

Pray = ARROZAR

Pray = ORASIONAR

Predict = ENDEVINAR

Predict = ENDIVINAR

Prepare = APAREJAR

Prepare = APRONTAR

Present = PREZENTAR

Preserve = KONSERVAR

Preserve = PREZERVAR

Proceed = PROVENIR

Produce = PRODUZIR

Produced, Have = AVER PRODUZIDO

Progress forth = PROGRESAR

Prohibit = DEFENDER

Prolong = PROLUNGAR

Promise = PROMETER

Pronounce = PRONUNSIAR

Prophesy = ENDEVINAR

Prophesy = ENDIVINAR

Propose = PROPOZAR

Protect oneself from the cold = ABRIGARSE

Protest = PROTESTAR

Prove = PREVAR

Prove = PROVAR

Publish = PUBLIKAR

Punch = AHARVAR

Punch = DAR PUNYO

Pursue = PERSEGUIR

Pursued, Have = AVER PERSEGUIDO

Push = ARREPUSHAR

Push = ARRONDJAR

Put = METER

Put = POZAR

Put in order = ORDENAR

Put, Have = AVER METIDO

Qualify = KALIFIKAR

Question = DEMANDAR

Question = PRUNTAR

Question = PREGUNTAR

Rain = AZER LUVYA

Rain = LUVIAR

Rained, Has = A LUVIADO

Raise = KRIAR

Reach = ALKANSAR

Reached, Have = AVER ALKANSADO

Read = MELDAR

Read, Have = AVER MELDADO

Realize = RENDERSE KUENTO

Receive = ARRESEVIR

Receive = RESIVIR

Received, Have = AVER ARRESEVIDO

Received, Have = AVER RESIVIDO

Reconsider = BADKAR

Recover = REKOVRAR

Recover = REKUPERAR

Recuperate = REKOVRAR

Recuperate = REKUPERAR

Reduce = ENCHIKESER

Regret = REGRETAR

Remain = KEDAR

Remained, Have = AVER KEDADO

Remember = AKODRAR

Remembered, Have = AVER AKODRADO

Remind = ENMENTAR

Renounce = ESVACHEARSE

Rent = ALKILAR

Repair = ADOVAR

Repair = REPARAR

Repeat = REPETAR

Repent = ARREPENTIRSE

Replicate = REPLIKAR

Resolve = REZOLVER

Respond = RESPONDER

Rest = DESKANSAR

Restore = RESTORAR

Return = TORNAR

Return = VOLVER

Return to = TORNAR I

Returned, Have = AVER TORNADO

Returned, Have = AVER VUELTO

Reunite = REUNIR

Reunite = REUNIRSE

Revive = ABIVIGUAR

Revolve = ABOLTAR

Revolve = MENEAR

Rise [of the sun] = AMANESER

Risk = RIZIKAR

Roar = GRITAR

Rob = ROVAR

Ruin = FALITAR

Rule as a King = ENREINAR

Run = KORER

Run = KORRER

Run, Have = AVER KORIDO

Run, Have = AVER KORRIDO

Said, Have = AVER DICHO / DICHU

Sat down, Have = AVER ASENTADOSE

Sat, Have = AVER ASENTADOSE

Save = GUADRAR

Save = SALVAR

Say = DEZIR

Scare = ESPANTAR

Scare = ESPANTARSE

Schmooze = ECHAR LASHON

Scrape = RAYAR

Scratch = ARRASKAR

Scratch oneself = ARRASKARSE

Search = BUSKHAR

Searched, Have = AVER BUSKHADO

See = VER

Seek = BUSKHAR

Seem = PARESER

Seen, Have = AVER VISTO

Seesaw = KUNARSE

Seize = APANYAR

Sell = VENDER

Sell = VENTER

Send = EMBIAR

Send = EMBIAR

Send = MANDAR

Sent, Have = AVER EMBIADO

Sent, Have = AVER MANDADO

Sew = KUZIR

Shake = MENEAR

Shake = TREMBLAR

Sharpen = AGUZAR

Shave = ARAPAR

Shave oneself = ARAPARSE

Shine = ARRELUMBRAR

Shine = BRIYAR

Shine = PARPAREAR

Shoot = TIRAR

Show = AMOSTRAR

Show off = PARPAREAR

Showed, Have = AVER AMOSTRADO

Shower = TOMAR DUSH

Shut = SERRAR

Shut up (stop the mouth) = KAYARSE

Shut, Have = AVER SERRADO

Signified, Have = AVER SIGNIFIKADO

Signify = SINYIFIKAR

Sing = KANTAR

Sit = ASENTARSE

Sit down = ASENTARSE

Slacken = AFLOSHAR

Sleep = DURMER

Sleep = DURMIR

Slept, Have = AVER DURMIDO

Smell = GOLER

Smile = SONREIR

Snack = MERENDAR

Snack = PIKNIKAR

Sold, Have = AVER VENTIDO

Sought, Have = AVER BUSKHADO

Sound = SONAR

Speak = AVLAR

Speak = FAVLAR

Speculate = ESPEKULAR

Spend = GASTAR

Spent, Have = AVER GASTADO

Spit = ESKUPIR

Splint = ENTAVLAR

Split up = ALESHAR

Spoken, Have = AVER AVLADO

Spoken, Have = AVER FAVLADO

Spread = DIFUZAR

Stand up = ALEVANTAR

Start = EMPESAR

Start = INISIAR

Started, Have = AVER EMPESADO

Stay = KEDAR

Stay = KEDARSE

Stayed, Have = AVER KEDADO

Stayed, Have = AVER KEDADOSE

Stew = GIZAR

Stop = ARRESTARSE

Stop = KEDARSE

Stop = KEDARSE

Stopped, Have = AVE KEDADOSE

Strike = AHARVAR

Stroke = KARESAR

Struggle = ESFORSARSE

Studied, Have = AVER ESTUDIADO

Study = ESTUDIAR

Submit = SOMETER

Suffer = SUFRIR

Suffocate = ATABAFAR

Suggest = SUGJERAR

Sung, Have = AVER KANTADO

Supose = SUPOZAR

Support = APOYAR

Support = ARRIMAR

Support = SUPORTAR

Support = SOMPORTAR

Surprise = SORPRENDER

Surround = ENTORNAR

Survive = SURVIVIR

Swear = DJURAR

Sweep = BARRIR

Swim = NADAR

Swing = KUNARSE

Take = TOMAR

Take = YEVAR

Take a shower = TOMAR DUSH

Take a walk = PASEAR

Take care of = KUDIAR

Taken = AVE TOMADO

Taken, Have = AVER YEVADO

Taught, Have = AVER ENSENYADO

Teach = ENSENYAR

Tell = DEZIR

Tell = DIZIR

Tell = KONTAR

Tell a story = KONTAR MAASÉ

Terminate = BITEREAR

Terminate = ATEMAR

Thank = AGRADESER

Think = PENSAR

Thought, Have = AVER PENSADO

Throw = ECHAR

Throw = LANSAR

Throw = TRAVAR

Tie up = ECHARSE ANYUDO

Told, Have = AVER DICHO / DICHU

Told, Have = AVER KONTADO

Touch = TOKAR

Translate = TRADUIZIR

Translate = TRESLADAR

Translate into Ladino = ENLADINAR

Translate into Ladino = LADINAR

Translated, Have = AVER TRADUZIDO

Travel = VIAJAR

Tread = OIZAR

Tread = PIZAR

Treat = TRATAR

Tried to, Have = AVER PERKURADO DE

Triumph = TRIUNFAR

Trouble = EMBARASAR

Trust = ENFEUZIAR

Trust = KONFIAR

Try = EKSPERIMENTAR

Try = PREVAR

Try = PROVAR

Try to = PERKURAR DE

Turn in = ENTREGAR

Turn on = ASENDER

Turn on = ENSENDER

Turn upside down = ABOLTAR

Understand = ENTENDER

Understood, Have = AVER ENTENDIDO

Unite = ADJUNTAR

Unite = AUNAR

Unite = UNIR

Use 'Tu' = TUTUAYAR

Use = UZAR

Used, Have = AVER UZADO

Vow = PROMETER

Wait = ESPERAR

Wait for = ASPERAR

Wait for = ESPERAR

Waited, Have = AVER ESPERADO

Wake up = DESPERTAR

Wake up = ESPERTARSE

Walk = KAMINAR

Walked, Have = AVER KAMINADO

Want = KERER

Wanted, Have = AVER KERIDO

Warn = AVERTIR

Wash = LAVAR

Wash himself = LAVARSE

Wash oneself = LAVARSE

Wash themselves = LAVARSEN

Washed, Have = AVER LAVADO

Watch = MIRAR

Watch over = GUADRAR

Wear = YEVARSE

Wet = MOJAR

Wield = MENEAR

Woken up, Have = AVER DESPERTADO

Work = LAVORAR

Worked, Have = AVER LAVORADO

Worry = PREOKUPARSE

Worry oneself = MERIKIARSE

Worry oneself = PERKURAR

Write = ESKRIVIR

Written, Have = AVER ESKRITO

Yearn = ESKARINYARSE

Part III: Useful Judeo-Spanish Phrases

This final section of the book is a collection of daily useful phrases in the Judeo-Spanish Language. The order of each line will follow the format of 'English < Judeo-Spanish' through its entirety. These phrases will be some of the most important phrases to know and use while traveling within Sephardic Jewish Communities around the World and we hope that they may someday be used by a curious traveler.

I)   Greetings & Farewells

Hello! – SHALOM!

Hello! – BUENOS DIYAS!

Welcome! –

BARUX ABÁ!

BARUH ABÁ!

VINIDO BUENO!

Good morning! –

BUENOS DIYAS!

BUENA DEMANYANA!

Good afternoon! –

BUENAS TARDES!

Good evening! –

BUENAS TARDES!

BUENA TADRADA!

Good night! –

BUENOS NOCHES!

Goodbye! –

ADYO!

AL VERMOS!

AU REVOIR!

KEDAVOS EN BUENORA!

May we speak later! May we speak again soon!

– PUEDEMOS AVLAR OTRA VEZ MAZ

TARDE?

See you soon! –

AL VERMOS!

Until tomorrow! –

ASTA DEMANYANA!

Let's grab a coffee! –

VAYAMOS A MERKAR UN CAVÉ!

Sorry! I can't –

LO SYENTO! NON PUEDO

Let's go! –

VAYAMOS! VAMOS! VAMONOS!

You look great today! –

TE VES BYEN OY!

You look great too! –

GRASYAS! I TE VES BYEN TAMBIÉN!

Excellent! –

EKSELENTE!

I am late for work –

YO SE TARDE AL LAVORO

Don't be late! –

NON TE VAYAS TARDE!

Hurry! –

APRESURATE!

TEN PRISA!

Good Luck! –

BUENA SUERTE!

Have a nice day! –

TENGA UN BUEN DIYA!

You are going to treat me to an ice cream! –

ME VAS A TRATAR UN AYISCRIN!

II)   Basic phrases of conversation

Yes – SI

No – NO

What's up? What's going on? –

KE PASA?

KE XABER?

KE HABER?

KE TAL?

How's it going with you? –

KOMO VA A TI?

KOMO VA A VOZÓS?

KE TAL ESTAS / ESTASH?

How are you? –

KOMO ESTAS?

KOMO ESTASH?

I'm well, thank you. –

BYEN, GRASYAS!

And you? How are you? –

I TU? KOMO ESTA?

I VOZOTROS? KOMO ESTASH?

I am well, as well –

ESTO BYEN, TAMBIÉN

Thank you very much! –

MERSÍ MUNCHO!

MUNCHAS GRASYAS!

Thank you! –

GRASYAS / GRASIAS!

MERCÍ!

You're Welcome –

DE NADA!

All is well –

TODO ESTA BYEN!

TODO VA BYEN!

What's your name? –

KOMO TE YAMAS?

KUALO ES TU NOMBRE?

KOMO VOS YAMASH?

My name is… -

ME YAMO…

MI NOMBRE ES…

Pleased to me you! –

ENKANTADO! [said by man]

ENKANTADA! [said by woman]

MUNCHO PLAZER!

ES PLAZER KONOSERTE!

ES PLAZER KONOSERVOS!

Where do you come from? –

DE ANDE VIENES TU?

DE ANDE VENISH VOZÓS!

Where are you from? –

DE ANDE SOS TU?

DE ANDE SOSH VOS?

I'm from the United States –

SE DE LOS ESTADOS UNIDOS

SE DE AMERIKA

I am from Israel –

SE DE YISRAEL / ISRAEL

How old are you? –

KUANTOS ANYOS TIENES / TENES TU?

KUANTOS ANYOS TENÉSH VOS?

I am … years old –

TENGO …ANYO [1] / ANYOS [2-100]

UNO – 1

DOS – 2

TREZ – 3

KUATRO – 4

SINKO – 5

SESH – 6

SYETE -7

OCHO – 8

MUEVE – 9

DYEZ – 10

ONZE – 11

DODJE – 12

TREDJE – 13

KATORDJE – 14

KINDJE – 15

DYEZISESH – 16

DYEZISYETE – 17

DYEZIOCHO – 18

DYEZIMUEVE – 19

VENTE – 20

VENTIUN – 21

VENTIDOS – 22

VENTITREZ – 23

VENTIKUATRO – 24

VENTISINKO – 25

VENTISESH – 26

VENTISYETE – 27

VENTIOCHO – 28

VENTIMUEVE – 29

TRENTA – 30

TRENTA I UNO – 31

TRENTA I DOS – 32

TRENTA I TREZ – 33

TRENTA I KUATRO – 34

TRENTA I SINKO – 35

KUARENTA – 40

SINKUENTA – 50

SESHENTA – 60

SETENTA – 70

OCHENTA – 80

MOVENTA – 90

ZIEN – 100

Please, Tell me that in English –

POR FAVOR, DIMELO EN INGLEZ!

POR FAVOR , DIZILDO EN INGLEZ!

Please say that again! –

POR FAVOR, DIMELO ANKORA!

POR FAVOR, DIZILDO ANKORA!

Do you speak Judeo-Spanish / Ladino? –

AVLAS DJUDEO-ESPANYOL / LADINO?

FAVLAS DJUDEO-ESPANYOL / LADINO?

AVLASH DJUDEO-ESPANYOL / LADINO?

FAVLASH DJUDEO-ESPANYOL / LADINO?

Yes, a little –

SI, UN POKO

I speak Judeo-Spanish / Ladino –

AVLO DJUDEO-ESPANYOL / LADINO

FAVLO DJUDEO-ESPANYOL / LADINO

I don't speak Judeo-Spanish / Ladino –

NON AVLO DJUDEO-ESPANYOL / LADINO

NON FAVLO DJUDEO-ESPANYOL / LADINO

I speak a little Judeo-Spanish / Ladino –

YO AVLO UN POKO DJUDEO-ESPANYOL / LADINO

YO FAVLO UN POKO DJUDEO-ESPANYOL / LADINO

Please Speak Slowly –

POR FAVOR, AVLA AVARIGO!

POR FAVOR AVLA LENTAMENTE!

POR FAVOR, FAVLA AVARIGO!

POR FAVOR, FAVLA LENTAMENTE!

Please, Tell me that again –

POR FAVOR, DIME ESTE OTRA VEZ!

POR FAVOR, REPETALO!

What do you want me to say? –

KI KERES KE YO DIGA?

KE KERÉSH VOS KE YO DIGA?

You talk too fast –

AVLAS DEMAZIADO RAPIDO

AVLASH DEMAZIADO RAPIDO

I'm sorry –

LO SYENTO!

DISKULPAME!

Forgive me! –

DISKULPAME!

DISKULPADME!

I forgive you –

TE DISKULPO

Do you forgive me? –

ME DISKULPAS TU?

ME DISKULPASH VOZÓS?

Do you understand? –

ENTIENDES? / ENTENDES?

ENTENDÉSH?

I don't understand –

NON ENTIENDO

Do you know? –

LO SAVES?

LO SAVÉSH?

You don't know? –

TU NON SAVES?

VOZOSTROS NON SAVÉSH?

No, I don't know =

NO! NO SE!

I don't want to know –

NO KERO SAVER

What happened? –

KE PASÓ?

KE AKONTESIÓ

Excuse me! –

EKSKUSA!

PARDON!

PERDON!

Go! –

VETE! VAYASE! VAYANSE!

Come here! –

VENTE AKI!

VENGASE AKI!

When did you arrive? –

KUANDO AYEGATES?

KUANDO AYEGATÉSH?

KUANDO ARRIVATES?

KUANDO ARRIVATÉSH?

I arrived yesterday / the day before yesterday –

ARRIVÍ / AYEGÍ AYER / ANITYER

I arrived today –

ARRIVÍ / AYEGÍ OY

What kind of work do you do? –

KE TIPO DE LAVORO AZES?

KE TIPO DE LAVORO AZÉSH?

I work as a… - LAVORO KOMO UN/UNA...

MASC. / FEM.

Accountant – KONTADOR / KONTADORA

Attorney – AVOKATO / AVOKATA

Baker – PANADERO / PANADERA

Businessman – EMPRESARIO / EMPRESARIA

Chef – SHEF

Doctor – DOKTOR / DOKTORA

Laborer – LAVORADOR / LAVORADORA

Lawyer – AVOKATO / AVOKATA

Salesman – VENDEDOR / VENTEDOR

Saleswoman – VENDEDORA / VENTEDORA

Student – ESTUDIANTE / ESTUDIANTA

Translator – TRADUKTOR / TRADUKTORA

Traveler – VIAJERO / VIAJERA

Where are you going? –

ANDE VAS?

ANDE VASH?

Where did you go? –

ANDE FUITES?

ANDE FUITÉSH?

Where are you all going? –

ANDE VAN TODOS LOS VOZOTROS?

Where did you all go? –

ANDE FUITÉSH / HUITÉSH TODOS LOS

VOZOTROS?

Who did you go with? –

KON KEN FUITES / HUITES TU?

I have to go –

TENGO KE IR

DEVO IR

I have to work –

TENGO KE LAVORAR

DEVO LAVORAR

I have to leave –

TENGO KE PARTIR

DEVO PARTIR

I have to do it –

TENGO KE AZERLO

DEVO AZERLO

I will return –

VO A TORNAR

I will return again –

VO A TORNAR OTRA VEZ

VO A TORNAR DE MUEVO

VO A TORNAR ANKORA

I will return tomorrow –

VO A TORNAR DEMANYANA

I will return next year –

VO A TORNAR EN OTRO ANYO

Where is the bank? –

ANDE ESTA EL BANKO?

Take me to the bank –

YEVEME AL BANKO!

I need to exchange a little money –

NESESITO TROKAR UN POKO PARAS

NESESITO TROKAR UN POKO MONEDA

I want to exchange money –

KERO TROKAR PARAS

KERO TROKAR MONEDA

Where is the market [store]? –

ANDE ESTA EL SUPERMARKET / SHARSHÍ?

Take me to the market –

YEVEME AL SUPERMARKET / SHARSHÍ!

I need to buy food –

NESESITO MERKAR KOMIDA

TENGO KE MERKAR KOMIDA

I need to buy fruit –

NESESITO MERKAR FRUTA

What is that? What is this? What is it? –

KE ES ESTE? KE TAL ES ESTE? KE ES AKEL?

How much does it (that) cost? –

KUANTO KOSTA ESTE?

KUANTO?

How much do I owe you? –

KUANTO TE DEVO?

I don't want to buy this –

NO KERO MERKAR ESTE

Yes, I want to buy it –

SI, KERO MERKAR ESTE

I'm sorry, I can't buy it –

LO SYENTO! NON LO PUEDO MERKAR

Is there something a lot cheaper? –

AY ALGO MAZ BARATO?

I don't have much money –

NO TENGO MUNCHA MONEDA

NO TENGO MUNCHAS PARAS

Do you accept credit card? –

AKSEPTE KARTAS DE KREDITO?

I want to use a credit card –

KERO UZAR UNA KARTA DE KREDITO

You can insert your credit card –

PUEDE ENKASHAR TU KARTA DE KREDITO

If I had sufficient money, I would buy it –

SI TUVIERA BASTANTE MONEDA, LO
MERKARÍA

I like it –

ME AGRADA

I don't like it –

NON ME AGRADA

What are you doing? –

KE AZES?

KE AZÉSH?

What will you do?

KE ARAS?

KE ARÉSH?

Where is there a store that sells…? –

ANDE AY UNA BODRUM / BOTIKA KE

VENDE / VENTE…?

Books – LIVROS

Clothing – ROPA

Electronics – ELEKTRONIKA

Food – KOMIDA

Fruit – FRUTA

Gifts – REGALOS

Ice cream – YELADO / AYISCRIN

Meat – CARNE

Shoes – CHAPINES

Toys – DJUGETES

I want to go to… –

KERO IR A…

We want to go to… –

KEREMOS IR A…

How much does it cost? –

KUANTO KOSTA?

I'm hungry –

TENGO AMBRE

I'm thirsty –

TENGO SER

Let's look for food –

BUSHKEMOS KOMIDA!

I need to use the restroom –

NESESITO UZAR EL BANYO

NESESITO UZAR LA TUALETA

Where is the bathroom? –

ANDE ESTA EL BANYO?

ANDE ESTA LA TUALETA?

Give me coffee please –

POR FAVOR, DAME UN KAVÉ

You are very beautiful / handsome –

TU SOS BYEN ERMOZA [to a girl]

TU SOS BYEN FERMOZA [to a girl]

VOZÓS SOSH BYEN ERMOZA [to a girl]

VOZÓS SOSH BYEN FERMOZA [to a girl]

TU SOS BYEN ERMOZO [to a man]

TU SOS BYEN FERMOZO [to a man]

VOZÓS SOSH BYEN ERMOZO [to a man]

VOZÓS SOSH BYEN FERMOZO [to a man]

You have a very cute face –

TU KARA ES LINDA

Can I take a photo? –

PUEDO TOMAR UNA FOTO?

Can I take a photo here or not? –

PUEDO TOMAR UNA FOTO AKI O NO?

Is there a hotel here? –

AY UN OTEL / MOTEL AKI?

Take me to the Hotel –

YEVEME AL OTEL / MOTEL!

Is there a room available in which I can stay / sleep? –

AY UN KAMARETA DISPONIVLE EN KUALA PUEDO KEDARME / DURMIR?

How many nights do you want to stay? –

KUANTOS NOCHES KERESH KEDARVOS AKI?

I want to stay here for one / two / three nights –

KERO KEDARME AKI [POR UNA NOCHE / POR DOS NOCHES / POR TREZ NOCHES]

How much does the room cost? –

KUANTO KOSTA LA KAMARETA?

Can I see the room? –

PUEDO VER LA KAMARETA?

I don't like it –

NON ME AGRADA

I like it, I'll take the room –

ME AGRADA, KERO LA KAMARETA

The room is dirty, I want a different one –

ESTA KAMARETA ES EMBATAKADA /
SUZIA, KERO OTRA KAMARETA

All of the sheets are dirty –

TODAS LAS SAVANAS SON
EMBATAKADAS / SUZIAS

Did you all sleep well? –

DURMITES BYEN?

DURMITÉSH BYEN?

I didn't sleep well –

NON DORMI BYEN

Why not? –

PORKE NO?

There was too much noise –

AVÍA DEMAZIADO MUNCHO BRUÍDO

I want to leave –

KERO SALIR

KERO PARTIR

Let's look for another hotel! –

BUSHKEMOS OTRO OTEL / OTRO MOTEL!

Do you want to go with me? –

KERES IR KON MI?

KERÉSH IR KON MI?

No, I can't go with you –

NO, NON PUEDO IR KON TI

No, I don't want to go with you –

NO, NON KERO IR KON TI / KON VOZOTROS

Can I help you? –

TE PUEDO AYUDAR?

I can't help you –

NO TE PUEDO AYUDAR

I want you to help me –

KERO KE ME AYUDES

If I had money, I would help you –

SI TUVIERA PARAS, TE AYUDARÍA

If I had money, I would leave –

SI TUVIERA PARAS, IRÍA YO

Why do you want to help me? –

PORKE ME KERES AYUDAR?

PORKE ME KERÉSH AYUDAR?

Is this yours? –

ES DE TÍ?

This is not yours –

ESTE NO ES DE TÍ

It's not mine –

NO ES DE MÍ

Yes, it's mine –

SI, ES DE MI

I hope you have a good day –

ISHALLA KE TENGAS UN BUEN DIYA!

ISHALLA KE TENGA UN BUEN DIYA!

I hope you can come –

ISHALLA PUEDAS VENIR

ISHALLA PUEDASH VENIR

I hope I can find it –

ISHALLA LO PUEDA TOPAR / ENKONTRAR

Hopefully it doesn't rain today –

ISHALLA NO VAYA A LUVIAR OY

Where is the Synagogue? –

ANDE ESTA EL KAL / KAHAL?

Take me to the Synagogue! –

YEVEME AL KAL / KAHAL!

YEVEME A LA KEILÁ / KEHILÁ!

Where is your house? –

ANDE ESTA TU KAZA?

God bless you –

DYO TE BENDIGA!

DYO VOS BENDIGA!

BERAXOT!

God bless you all –

DYO LOS BENDIGA A TODOS LOS

VOZOTROS!

Let's pray for this food –

VAMOS A ORASIONAR POR LA KOMIDA!

ORASIONEMOS POR LA KOMIDA!

I love you –

TE AMO [with one's partner]

TE KERO [with family]

Do you love me? –

¿ME AMAS?

¿ME AMASH?

I want to kiss you –

TE KERO BEZAR

I want to hug you –

TE KERO ABRAZAR

I will miss you very much –

TE VO A ECHAR MUNCHO DE MANKO

TE VO A ECHAR MUNCHO DE MENOS

I have missed you –

TE AVO ECHADO MUNCHO DE MANKO

TE AVO ECHADO MUNCHO DE MENOS

I miss you –

TE ECHO MUNCHO DE MANKO

TE ECHO MUNCHO DE MENOS

I will never forget you –

NUNKA TE VO A OLVIDAR

NO TE VO A OLVIDAR NUNKA

I only want to stay at your side –

SOLO KERO KEDARME A TU LADIKO

Take me to the airport –

YEVEME AL AEROPUERTO / SADÁ TE'UFÁ!

I need a taxi –

NESESITO TAKSI

I am at the airport –

ESTO EN EL AEROPUERTO / SADÁ TE'UFÁ

Get in! [the car] –

SUBETE!

I am going to wait here –

VO A ESPERAR AKI

Let's Celebrate! –

SELEBREMOS!

Happy New Year! –

FELIS ANYO MUEVO!

Merry Christmas! –

NOEL ALEGRE!

Happy Birthday! –

FELIS ANIVERSARIO!

Happy Sabbath! –

BUEN SHABAT!

Happy Passover! –

BUEN PESAH!

III)   COMMON COMMANDS [Imperatives]:

Go! –

VETE! VAYASE! VAYANSE!

Come here! –

VENTE AKI!

VEN AKI!

VENID AKI!

Come with me! –

VENTE KON MI!

VENID KON MI!

Let's go!!! –

VAMOS! VAYAMOS! VAMONOS!

Let's eat!!! –

KOMEMOS!

VAMOS A KOMER!

Let's work!!! –

LAVOREMOS!

VAMOS A LAVORAR!

Do it!!! –

AZLO! AGALO! AGANLO!

Don't do it! –

NON LO AGAS! NON LO AGA!

Do me a favor, Please! –

AGAME UN FAVOR, POR FAVOR!

Let's do it!!! –

AGAMOSLO!

Let's dance!!! –

BAYLEMOS!

VAMOS A BAYLAR!

Give me it!!! –

DAMELO!

Give me two beers, Please –

DAME DOS BIRAS, POR FAVOR!

Please give me a glass of water –

DAME UNA TAZA DE AGUA, POR FAVOR!

Please bring me a cup of tea! –

DAME UNA TAZA / KOS DE CHAY

KAYENTE, POR FAVOR!

Please bring me a cup of coffee! –

DAME UNA TAZA / KOS DE KAVÉ, POR

FAVOR

Drink! – BEVE! / BEVA!

Drink water! – BEVA AGUA!

Don't touch me! –

NO ME TOKES!

Enter! Come in! –

ENTRATE! ENTRESE! ENTRENSE!

Open / Close the door / the window! –

AVRE / SERRA LA PUERTA / LA VENTANA!

Welcome to my home –

BUEN VENIDO A MI KAZA!

Wait for me here! –

ESPERAME AKI!

ESPEREME AKI!

Take me to the market! –

YEVEME AL SHARSHÍ!

YEVEME AL SUPERMARKET!

Buy it! –

MERKALO!

Bring it to me! –

TRAIGAMELO!

TRAIGANMELO!

Guide me there! –

ORIENTAME ASTA AYA!

ORIENTEME ASTA AYA!

IV) EMERGENCY PHRASES:

Help me! –

AYUDAME! AYUDEME! AYUDENME!

Be Careful!!! –

TEN KUDIADO!

ECHA TINE!

Don't Fall!!! –

NO TE KAIGAS!

Don't mess with me!!! –

NO ME MOLESTES!

NON ME FISHUGES!

Call the Police! –

YAME LA POLIS!

YAME LA POLISIYA!

Do it!!! – AGALO!

Someone robbed me –

ALGO ME ROVÓ

Someone stole my things –

ALGO AVE ROVADO MIS KOZAS

Where is the Hospital? –

ANDE ESTA EL OSPITAL?

A dog bit me –

UN PERRO ME MORDIO

A snake bit me –

UNA KULEVRA ME MORDIO

I'm bleeding very bad –

ESTO SANGRANDO MUNCHO

I was bleeding very bad –

ESTAVA SANGRANDO MUY MAL

I need water –

NESESITO AGUA

I'm sick –

ESTO HAZINO [m.]

ESTO HAZINA [f.]

I'm pregnant –

ESTO PRENYADA [said only by women]

I am in a lot of pain –

TENGO TANTO DOLOR

TENGO MUNCHO DOLOR

I cannot walk –

NO PUEDO KAMINAR

My ... hurts – (...) ME ERGUELE MUNCHO

Anus = EL ANO

Arm = EL BRAZO

Back = LA ESPALDA

Breast = LA TETA

Chest = EL PECHO

Ear = LA OREJA / EL OÍDO

Eye; Eyes = EL OJO / LOS OJOS

Face = LA KARA

Finger = EL DEDO

Foot = LA PIE

Hand = LA MANO

Head = LA KAVESA

Heart = EL KORASON

Leg = LA PIERNA

Lip(s) = LOS MUSHOS

Mouth = LA BOKA

Nose = LA NARIZ

Penis = EL PENE

Shoulder = EL OMBRO

Stomach = EL ESTOMAGO

Throat = LA GARGANTA

Toe = EL DEDO DE PIE

Tongue = LA LINGUA

Tooth; Teeth = EL DIENTE / LOS DIENTES

Vagina = LA VAGINA

I have diarrhea –

TENGO DIARREA

I have diarrhea and vomiting –

TENGO DIARREA Y VOMITO MUNCHO

I'm afraid –

TENGO MIEDO

TENGO ESPANTO

I was afraid –

TENÍA MORÁ

TENÍA ESPANTO

Don't be afraid –

NO TENGAS MORÁ!

NO TENGAS ESPANTO!

Take me to the Hospital –

YEVEME AL OSPITAL!

Please, Come with me! –

POR FAVOR, VENTE KON MI!

V)   NUMBERS

ZERO – 0

MEDIO – ½

UNO – 1

DOS – 2

TREZ – 3

KUATRO – 4

SINKO – 5

SESH – 6

SYETE -7

OCHO – 8

MUEVE – 9

DYEZ – 10

ONZE – 11

DODJE – 12

TREDJE – 13

KATORDJE – 14

KINDJE – 15

DYEZISESH – 16

DYEZISYETE – 17

DYEZIOCHO – 18

DYEZIMUEVE – 19

VENTE – 20

VENTIUN – 21

VENTIDOS – 22

VENTITREZ – 23

VENTIKUATRO – 24

VENTISINKO – 25

VENTISESH – 26

VENTISYETE – 27

VENTIOCHO – 28

VENTIMUEVE – 29

TRENTA – 30

TRENTA I UNO – 31

TRENTA I DOS – 32

TRENTA I TREZ – 33

TRENTA I KUATRO – 34

TRENTA I SINKO – 35

KUARENTA – 40

SINKUENTA – 50

SESHENTA – 60

SETENTA – 70

OCHENTA – 80

MOVENTA – 90

ZIEN – 100

ZIENTO VENTISINKO – 125

ZIENTO SINKUENTA – 150

ZIENTO SETENTA I SINKO – 175

DOZIENTOS – 200

TREZIENTOS – 300

KUATROZIENTOS – 400

KINYENTOS – 500

SEZIENTOS – 600

SYETEZIENTOS – 700

OCHOZIENTOS – 800

MOVEZIENTOS – 900

UN MIL – 1000

DOS MIL – 2000

TREZ MIL – 3000

KUATRO MIL – 4000

SINKO MIL – 5000

ZIEN MIL – 100,000

DOZIENTOS MIL – 200,000

UN MILYON – 1,000,000

UN MIL MILYONES – 1,000,000,000

COMMON JUDEO-SPANISH SAYINGS:

KAPARA! =

IT COULD BE WORSE!

DJENTE DE PIRON =

THE ONE PERCENT – "PEOPLE OF THE FORK"

HADRAS I BARANAS! =

BIG FUSS!

ENGLENEATE! =

HAVE FUN!

LAS ANYADAS NON AZEN SEZUDOS, ELLAS NON AZEN KE VIEJOS =

THE YEARS DON'T MAKE PEOPLE WISE, THEY JUST MAKE THEM OLD

KUANDO SE ESKURESE ES PARA AMANESER =

WHEN IT IS DARK OUT THAT'S BECAUSE THE DAWN IS COMING

TODOS LOS DEDOS DE LA MANO NO SON UNOS =

ALL THE FINGERS OF THE HAND ARE NOT THE SAME

Resources:

Field Research of the Judeo-Spanish Language

Conducted by Matthew Grant Russo

Source: Notes taken by Mateo G. Russo of the Judeo-Spanish Language from Feb 2023 to March 2023 from conversations with Native Speakers; especially through youtube.com. The Native-speaker resource was: Uriel Medina.

In Person and Online.

Other Publications and Books by Author:

[B'ajlom ii Nkotz'i'j Publications and KDP Publishing]

"B'ajlom ii Nkotz'i'j Publications' Tz'utujiil Maya Phrasebook: Ideal for Traveling in Sololá, Guatemala C.A., 3rd Edition" (2019)

"B'ajlom ii Nkotz'i'j Publications' Ch'ol Maya Phrasebook: Ideal for Traveling in Tumbalá, Chiapas, México, 2nd Edition" (2018)

"B'ajlom ii Nkotz'i'j Publications' Yucatec Maya (Maayat'aan) Phrasebook: Ideal for Traveling in Península de Yucatán, México, 2nd Edition" (2018)

"B'ajlom ii Nkotz'i'j Publications' Kazakh Phrasebook: Ideal for Traveling throughout Kazakhstan, 1st Edition" (2020)

"B'ajlom ii Nkotz'i'j Publications' K'iche' Maya Phrasebook: Ideal for Traveling throughout Guatemala, Central America, 1st Edition" (2020)

"B'ajlom ii Nkotz'i'j Publications' Bosnian Phrasebook: Ideal for Traveling throughout Bosnia & Herzegovina, 1st Edition" (2020)

"B'ajlom ii Nkotz'i'j Publications' Haitian Creole Phrasebook: Ideal for Traveling throughout Haiti, 1st Edition" (2020)

"B'ajlom ii Nkotz'i'j Publications' Kyrgyz Phrasebook: Ideal for Traveling throughout Kyrgyzstan, 1ˢᵗ Edition" (2020)

"B'ajlom ii Nkotz'i'j Publications' Luxembourgish Phrasebook: Ideal for Traveling throughout Luxembourg, 1ˢᵗ Edition" (2020)

"B'ajlom ii Nkotz'i'j Publications' German Phrasebook: Ideal for Traveling throughout Germany, 1ˢᵗ Edition" (2020)

"B'ajlom ii Nkotz'i'j Publications' Russian Phrasebook: Ideal for Traveling throughout the Russian Federation, 1ˢᵗ Edition" (2020)

"B'ajlom ii Nkotz'i'j Publications' Kurdish Phrasebook: Ideal for Traveling in Kurdistan, 1ˢᵗ Edition" (2020)

"B'ajlom ii Nkotz'i'j Publications' Yezidi Phrasebook: Ideal for Traveling within Yezidi Communities around the World, 1ˢᵗ Edition" (2020)

"B'ajlom ii Nkotz'i'j Publications' Classical & Modern Nahuatl Phrasebook: Ideal for Traveling throughout Central México, 1ˢᵗ Edition" (2020)

"B'ajlom ii Nkotz'i'j Publications' Catalan Phrasebook: Ideal for Traveling throughout Northeastern Spain, 1ˢᵗ Edition" (2020)

"B'ajlom ii Nkotz'i'j Publications' Galician Phrasebook: Ideal for Traveling throughout Northwestern Spain, 1ˢᵗ Edition" (2020)

"B'ajlom ii Nkotz'i'j Publications' Quechua Phrasebook: Ideal for Traveling in the Andean Regions of South America, 1ˢᵗ Edition" (2020)

"B'ajlom ii Nkotz'i'j Publications' Guatemalan Spanish Phrasebook: Ideal for Traveling throughout Guatemala, 1ˢᵗ Edition" (2020)

"B'ajlom ii Nkotz'i'j Publications' Guide to Classical Syriac, 1ˢᵗ Edition" (2020)

"B'ajlom ii Nkotz'i'j Publications' Guide to Coptic, 1ˢᵗ Edition" (2020)

"B'ajlom ii Nkotz'i'j Publications' Guide to Coptic: Revised Edition, 1ˢᵗ Edition" (2022)

"B'ajlom ii Nkotz'i'j Publications' A Linguistic Guide to Hebrew, Aramaic, Syriac & Arabic, 1ˢᵗ Edition" (2021)

"B'ajlom ii Nkotz'i'j Publications' A Linguistic Guide to Hebrew, Aramaic, Syriac & Arabic: Version 2.0, 1ˢᵗ Edition" (2021)

"B'ajlom ii Nkotz'i'j Publications' Guide to Jewish Babylonian Aramaic, 1ˢᵗ Edition" (2021)

"B'ajlom ii Nkotz'i'j Publications' Guide to Jewish Palestinian Aramaic, 1ˢᵗ Edition (2021)

"B'ajlom ii Nkotz'i'j Publications' Guide to Galilean Aramaic, 1ˢᵗ Edition" (2021)

"A Comparison of Four Mayan Languages: From México to Guatemala, 1ˢᵗ Edition" (2020)

"A Comparison of Four Mayan Languages: From México to Guatemala, Version 2.0, 1ˢᵗ Edition" (2021)

"B'ajlom ii Nkotz'i'j Publications' A Classical Syriac Dictionary with Basic Grammar, 1ˢᵗ Edition" (2021)

"B'ajlom ii Nkotz'i'j Publications' A Concise Syriac and Aramaic Dictionary, 1ˢᵗ Edition" (2021)

"B'ajlom ii Nkotz'i'j Publications' Concise Classical Syriac Dictionary, 1ˢᵗ Edition" (2022)

"B'ajlom ii Nkotz'i'j Publications' Persian Phrasebook: Ideal for Traveling in Iran, 1ˢᵗ Edition" (2022)

"B'ajlom ii Nkotz'i'j Publications' Dari Phrasebook: Ideal for Traveling in Afghanistan, 1ˢᵗ Edition" (2022)

"B'ajlom ii Nkotz'i'j Publications' Arabic Phrasebook: Ideal for Traveling to the Middle East, 1ˢᵗ Edition" (2022)

"B'ajlom ii Nkotz'i'j Publications' Hebrew Phrasebook: Ideal for Traveling to Israel, 1ˢᵗ Edition" (2022)

"B'ajlom ii Nkotz'i'j Publications' Guide to Hebrew, 1ˢᵗ Edition" (2022)

"B'ajlom ii Nkotz'i'j Publications' Mayan Glyph Coloring Book: Book 1, 1ˢᵗ Edition" (2022)

"B'ajlom ii Nkotz'i'j Publications' Mayan Glyph Coloring Book: Book 2, 1ˢᵗ Edition" (2022)

"An Aramaic Christian Rite of Exorcism: For the Cleansing of the Household and the Banishment of Demons, 1ˢᵗ Edition" (2022)

"B'ajlom ii Nkotz'i'j Publications' Guide to Classical Syriac: Extended Version, 1ˢᵗ Edition" (2022)

"B'ajlom ii Nkotz'i'j Publications' A Concise Classical Syriac Dictionary: 2ⁿᵈ Edition" (2023)

"B'ajlom ii Nkotz'i'j Publications' Classical Syriac – English Extended Dictionary: Volume I: Alaph – Mem, 1ˢᵗ Edition" (2023)

"B'ajlom ii Nkotz'i'j Publications' Classical Syriac – English Extended Dictionary: Volume II: Mem – Ayn, 1ˢᵗ Edition" (2023)

"B'ajlom ii Nkotz'i'j Publications' Classical Syriac – English Extended Dictionary: Volume III: AYN – TAW, 1ˢᵗ Edition" (2022)

"B'ajlom ii Nkotz'i'j Publications' Yucatec Maya Phrasebook: Special Edition, 1ˢᵗ Edition" (2023)

"B'ajlom ii Nkotz'i'j Publications' Guide to Arabic, 1ˢᵗ Edition" (2023)

"B'ajlom ii Nkotz'i'j Publications' Icelandic Phrasebook: Ideal for Traveling throughout Iceland, 1ˢᵗ Edition" *(2023)*

"B'ajlom ii Nkotz'i'j Publications' Yiddish Phrasebook: Ideal for Traveling in Jewish Communities around the World, 1ˢᵗ Edition (2023)

"B'ajlom ii Nkotz'i'j Publications' Corsican Phrasebook: Ideal for Traveling to Corsica, 1ˢᵗ Edition" *(2023)*

"B'ajlom ii Nkotz'i'j Publications' Romansh Phrasebook: Ideal for Traveling through the Swiss Canton of the Grisons, 1ˢᵗ Edition" *(2023)*

"B'ajlom ii Nkotz'i'j Publications' Sicilian Phrasebook: Ideal for Traveling to Sicily, 1ˢᵗ Edition" *(2023)*

"B'ajlom ii Nkotz'i'j Publications' Maltese Phrasebook: Ideal for Traveling to Malta, 1ˢᵗ Edition" *(2023)*

"B'ajlom ii Nkotz'i'j Publications' Slovenian Phrasebook: Ideal for Traveling to Slovenia, 1ˢᵗ Edition" *(2023)*

"B'ajlom ii Nkotz'i'j Publications' Slovak Phrasebook: Ideal for Traveling to Slovakia, 1ˢᵗ Edition" *(2023)*

"B'ajlom ii Nkotz'i'j Publications' Kaqchikel Maya Phrasebook: Ideal for Traveling to the Sololá Region of Guatemala, 1ˢᵗ Edition" *(2023)*

All publications are available on Amazon.com and Booksamillion.com

B'ajlom ii Nkotz'i'j Publications ™

FOR ANY QUESTIONS FEEL FREE TO CONTACT US AT:

Biinpublications@gmail.com

Printed in Great Britain
by Amazon